MEDIEVAL CELEBRATIONS

How to Plan Holidays, Weddings, and Reenactments with Recipes, Customs, Costumes, Decorations, Songs, Dances, and Games

DANIEL DIEHL and MARK DONNELLY

STACKPOLE
BOOKS

Copyright © 2001 by Daniel Diehl and Mark Donnelly

Published by
STACKPOLE BOOKS
5067 Ritter Road
Mechanicsburg, PA 17055
www.stackpolebooks.com

Printed in the United States of America

10 9 8 7 6 5 4 3 2 1

First Edition

Cover design by Caroline Stover
Front cover photos by Dick Clark, Peter Samworth, and Steve Lund
Interior photos by Daniel Diehl unless otherwise noted

Library of Congress Cataloging-in-Publication Data

Diehl, Daniel.
    Medieval Celebrations : how to plan holidays, weddings, and
reenactments with recipes, customs, costumes, decorations,
songs, dances, and games / Daniel Diehl and Mark Donnelly.—
1st ed.
        p. cm.
    Includes bibliographical references and index.
    ISBN 0-8117-2866-8
    1. Festivals. 2. Medievalism. 3. Manners and customs.
4. Social History—Medieval, 500–1500. I. Donnelly, Mark,
1967– II. Title.

GT3932 .D44 2001
394.2694'09'02—dc11
                            00-049682

TO EVERY GROWNUP
WHO STILL ENJOYS DRESSING UP.

Contents

PREFACE

Most of us are aware of the harsh realities of medieval life. The feudal period was fraught with political turmoil, brutal and incessant warring, random violence, unsanitary living conditions, and disease. Medieval life, as described by Thomas Hobbes, was "nasty, brutish and short." Despite this, there are few images more appealing than a magnificently armored knight riding out in the name of his lady, his king, and the church, to do battle against the forces of evil. Who among us does not long to change places with one of those glorious warriors from the past?

For centuries, chivalry and knightly honor have been popular literary themes. In the nineteenth century, medieval tournaments were recreated by the nobles and gentry of England and Europe. More recently, kings, knights, and courtly love have been constant themes in the theater and on television. About four decades ago, a few people brave enough to risk being mocked by their neighbors actually began recreating medieval life on a regular basis. It was a bold step backward.

Over the ensuing decades, the recreation of medieval feasts, tournaments, and fairs has increased tremendously in popularity. The romance of escaping, at least for a few hours, from the stress-filled, work-a-day world can be very attractive and a lot of fun. Beyond question, it can help make a special occasion even more memorable. A wedding with people dressed in fairy-tale clothes or a Christmas party with minstrels and a table groaning under the weight of strange and rich-smelling food will always be remembered as something spectacular, daring, and magical.

To those of you who feel the attraction of diving head-long into the past but really don't know where to begin, this book is for you.

ACKNOWLEDGMENTS

We owe a great debt of gratitude to a tremendous number of people for their help in making this book possible.

To illustrate recreated medieval celebrations, we have relied on people throughout the United States and England to donate photographs of their feasts and weddings. We hope that these pictures help our readers realize just how well the feeling of the Middle Ages can be brought to life with a little effort. For contributing these photos, we would like to thank Sean and Ingrid Clouter, Brian Edwards Photography, the York Archaeological Trust and Dr. Peter Addyman at Barley Hall, Dick Clark of Mayhem Photographics, Steve Lund and Tim Finkas for tracking him down, Peter and Theresa Samworth, and Robert Whitehouse.

Thanks also to Keith Piggott for donating the use of the Robyn Hode play; Martin Watts of the Ryedale Folk Museum for the rules for Merrills; Theakstons Brewery for the rules of Dice; David Bynham-Trousdale, Chris Thorne, Stuart Tonnar, and Angi Haywood for songs and music; Brenda Rich for advising us on costume patterns; and Kevin Bullimore for the use of the twelfth-century Sarum mass, songs, and so much other help. Thanks to Father Barry Williams for his kindness, help, and intimate knowledge of medieval Latin. And a very special thank-you to Paul Blackwell for his marvelous work on the dance chapter.

Finally, we want to thank Kyle Weaver and Amy Cooper at Stackpole Books for their faith and patience.

CHAPTER 1
GETTING STARTED

The popularity of recreating medieval celebrations has been encouraged and promoted by the Christmas madrigal dinners hosted by many civic and church organizations across the United States, England, and Europe. Likewise, the popularity of hundreds of Renaissance Fairs held throughout the United States and the rise of medieval reenactment groups around the globe have helped broaden the appeal of selectively recreating the "Age of Chivalry." The more one sees of this long-gone age, recreated by people who are, by and large, just like the rest of us, the more it seems like a great way to spend some free time. In fact, it is even more fun to take part in one of these medieval events than it is to attend them purely as a spectator. Even if you have never hosted a party before and your knowledge of the Middle Ages is limited to a few old Robin Hood movies, you can host a medieval banquet, with the aid of this book, that no one is likely to forget. And there are enough historical tidbits thrown into this book that by the day of your banquet you will sound like an authority on medieval history.

The truth of the matter is, with a little effort, a sense of adventure, and not much more money than it would cost to host any other type of party, you can successfully mount a beautiful and memorable medieval feast.

The Middle Ages, in its greater historical aspect, is a vaguely defined period of time. Historians endlessly argue when it began, when it ended, and even what, exactly, it was. For the sake of simplicity, we will define the Middle Ages as the period between 1066, when the Normans conquered England, and 1450, when the Renaissance and the rise of the nation-state brought an end to the feudal system that dominated the period. Basically, this gives us three and a half centuries to play with.

For a variety of practical reasons, we will be using an amalgam of styles, manners, and foods from this period to create our medieval feast. Because few written recipes from the early years of this period survive, we will extract our menu items primarily from cookbooks of the fourteenth and fifteenth centuries (1300s and 1400s). The clothing styles and decorative motifs covered in our chapters on costumes and decorating are taken primarily from the fourteenth century because they are far simpler, and therefore easier to reproduce, than those of the later Middle Ages. Our selection of music and dance comes from a variety of times and places throughout the medieval period. So while the variety of time periods on which we have drawn might drive a hard-nosed historian mad, and a visitor from the real Middle Ages would have no idea what was going on, our feast will be relatively simple for anyone to produce and is still based entirely in historical fact. For the sake of convenience, we will pretend that the feast takes place around the year 1350; at least this gives us a date to focus on.

The major concern most people have about attempting to recreate a medieval banquet has to do with food preparation. "How hard is it to make these things?" and "Will anyone eat them when they are served?" are both legitimate concerns to anyone contemplating hosting a medieval feast.

Most people, at most times throughout history, tend to eat foods with which they are familiar. The ingredients are available without undue hassle or expense, and the necessary preparation does not require learning a lot of new skills. When it's time to host a party, the best and favorite dishes become potential menu items. A little extra effort may go into the preparation and presentation, but no one wants to be a human guinea pig for some experimental cuisine. Likewise, the manners, customs, and decorations at a social event are not usually from some unaccustomed land; everyone will be on his or her best behavior at a feast, but no one wants to deal with strange customs and habits that feel awkward and uncomfortable. Consequently, throughout the course of this book, we will try to guide you, the reader and potential host, through the ins and outs of medieval customs and cooking in such a way that you can host a party based on the habits and foods of six centuries ago with confidence that you and your guests will feel comfortable and completely at ease with the results.

WHERE DO I START?

We have arranged this book in such a way that it can be equally useful to those readers who are planning a small dinner party, a large wedding, or a public event sponsored by a church or charity organization. We will help you gauge your medieval celebration to the size of the space in which you are holding it, the number of people who will be attending, and your budgetary constraints. We will aid you in planning, decorating, and organizing your kitchen to make your banquet as worry free as possible. Our hope is that when the big day comes, all of your guests will come to the feast ready to immerse themselves in the atmosphere of the "Age of Chivalry."

We will help you put together an information packet that will explain the day's events to your guests. The packet should include a copy of the menu; the exotic dishes often prove irresistible to those with an adventurous palate. Photocopy the chapter on medieval table manners to help your guests get into the mood of things. If your guests are expected to come in costume—and it is always more fun and more authentic if they do—they will need time to either make or rent appropriate clothing. You can provide copies of the clothing patterns in this book to anyone who expresses an interest in making his or her own costume.

If you are planning a medieval dinner in conjunction with a civic organization, such as a church, club, or charity organization, it will probably be impossible to get everyone to come in costume, but all should be encouraged to dress for the occasion if they so desire. If you hold similar events in coming years, you will almost certainly find the number who come in costume will increase from year to year. The costumes may not be authentic, but it will show that people are willing to get into the spirit of things and really enjoy themselves.

In addition to recipes, decorations, and costumes, this book provides information and instructions on a variety of games, dances, songs, and entertainments that will keep your guests enjoying themselves for an evening or an entire day. While all the basic information for a medieval feast, large or small, is contained in this book, for those of you who really want to go over the top or simply want to find more information about medieval celebrations, there is an extensive reference section and a bibliography at the back of the book. But even without referencing these additional sources, you should be able to prepare and host a medieval feast that will be remembered and talked about for years to come.

Allow yourself plenty of time to prepare your feast. You will probably want to read this entire book several times before you actually begin making final plans. If you are going all out, it can take two or three months of planning and preparation, followed by several weeks of hard work. Just take your time, don't panic, and above all, enjoy yourself. Be warned—these medieval banquets have a way of becoming a habit; soon after your first feast, you will find yourself thinking up ways of doing it better the next time.

CHAPTER 2
EDIEVAL CELEBRATIONS

◆

There is no such thing as a "typical" medieval celebration. Celebrations and feasts during the Middle Ages were as different and varied, for much the same reasons, as celebrations at any period of history, including our own. What might have seemed an immense and impressive celebration to village peasants would have been an appalling and miserable display to the eyes of great nobility. Consequently, before recreating a medieval feast, it's a good idea to first look at how different levels of society celebrated.

The vast majority of the medieval population were peasants; certainly more than 90 percent of them worked the land. While some of these peasants had incomes that were comfortable by their standards, and others lived among the sophisticated denizens of cities and towns, peasant life was never grand nor sophisticated. Neither was it healthy or sanitary.

Most peasants lived in small villages attached to a manor house or the estate of a lord. They made their living as sharecroppers, donating a portion of their labor and produce to the lord as payment for their rent and taxes. These villages were seldom more than a cluster of extended families held together by their social and economic isolation. With no means of transportation other than walking, it was a rare occasion when anyone left the village. Most people never traveled more than seven miles from the spot where they were born. Why seven miles? Because that is how far

one can travel on foot and safely return home by nightfall. Everyone in the village knew everyone else, and their business. Consequently, when someone in the village had a reason to celebrate, the entire village joined in.

The backbreaking demands of subsistence farming and the requirements of the feudal system meant that feasts were few and far between. When they did take place, they probably lasted only one day, usually a Sunday, when most work was suspended anyway. The only way more than one day could be taken away from work was if the lord decreed a public holiday. But such occasions were rare. When a feast was planned by and for the village, everyone pitched in to make certain the festivities came together, so the day would be as memorable as possible. In most villages, bread and ale were plentiful, as were fish, chicken, small birds, cheese, a stew of whatever vegetables were locally available and in season, and maybe the occasional pig or sheep, if the occasion were important enough. A cow was too valuable to kill just for a party, and wild game, with the exception of rabbits, was the exclusive property of the nobility.

Other than a church or chapel, there were few, if any, public buildings in a medieval village. Consequently, feasts and celebrations were normally held in the summer so they could take place outdoors. If anyone in the village knew how to play an instrument, he or she might provide music, but this, too, was fairly rare. Communal singing, on the other hand, was fairly common. Most of the songs were either religious in nature or appallingly bawdy. The event being celebrated—and how much ale had been consumed—dictated what sort of song would be sung at any particular point in time. Once the ale was gone and everyone had sung his song, told his story, or danced his dance—which everyone in the village had probably seen and heard a dozen times before—all went home. They had little choice; they had to be up at sunrise, ready to go to work.

At the opposite end of the social spectrum was the world of royalty, great nobles, archbishops, and bishops. Only on rare occasions did they have to cut their celebrations short because they had to go to work in the morning. In this world, great feasts, grand celebrations, glorious tournaments, and the presentation of lavish gifts were not only commonplace, they were also an important part of keeping a firm grip on power.

In the medieval world, hard cash, even among the most powerful, was almost nonexistent. Edward the Confessor, an Anglo-Saxon king of England, reputedly kept the entire royal treasury in a chest under his bed. Society functioned largely on barter, loyalty, feudal duty to the overlord, and fear of punishment from God or the Crown. The only effective way to display wealth and power was to keep up a good front, and hosting great feasts and tournaments was an ideal way of showing off. By bringing together political allies, potential allies, and even the occasional enemy, the nobility could reinforce and display their social and political strength. The larger the display, the greater the appearance of power.

Because travel during the Middle Ages was difficult at best, it was a rare occasion when any number of noblemen and ladies had the opportunity to get together and relax. A gathering of nobles, whether it be for military or purely social purposes, was an opportunity to celebrate and provided just cause for staging grand hunts, dancing, and feasts.

The guests at noble banquets were seated strictly according to rank and power. The highest-ranking personages, including the host, hostess, most powerful guests, and highest-ranking clergy, were seated around a "high table" strategically placed at the front of the great hall, in full view of the assembled company. Chairs were traditionally placed on only one side of the high table so that the rest of the room had an unobstructed view of the great and powerful. Some high tables were even placed on a raised platform, or dais, to improve the view of those seated there. If there were guests of greater rank than the hosts at the high table, they would be granted the honor of being seated at the center of the table. The most honored among the company were provided massive, high-backed armchairs. Those next in rank would have armchairs with lower backs, and toward the end of high table were chairs with no arms.

Other tables in the hall were usually arranged in long rows, at a ninety-degree angle to the high table, so guests could look down the length of their table toward the high table. Even at these lower tables, seating was all important; the closer a person was to the high table, the greater his rank and status. Those nearest the high table often had small, armless chairs; farther along were individual stools; and finally, at the far end of the hall, were common benches known as *bankettes*, from which the modern term *banquet* is derived. Beyond the tables was floor seating for musicians, entertainers, honored tradesmen, personal servants, and a few peasants that might have been invited to the feast as an act of Christian charity.

The food was also distributed according to rank. The best dishes, the greatest number of dishes, and the finest wines went to the high table, which was always served before the rest of the company. This allowed the guests to ooh and aah at the grandeur enjoyed by those of great rank.

Food was always served in a number of courses, called *removes*, or *messes* (a term still used in the military). There might be three, four, or even five removes, and each remove was a minibanquet in itself. The food was grand, gloriously prepared and presented, and seemingly available in endless quantity. The larger the occasion and the more powerful the hosts, the more impressive the results were likely to be. When England's King Henry III threw a Christmas banquet in 1246, the shopping list included five thousand chickens, eleven hundred partridges, four hundred hares and rabbits, ten thousand eels, thirty-six swans, fifty-four peacocks, and ninety boars. All of this would have gone to the royal butchers, then to the kitchens, there to be transformed into hundreds of impressive dishes, and finally taken to the tables of the revelers in what was probably a series of at least four or five removes. Because no one could possibly eat the amount of food that flowed through the great hall, guests took small portions so as not to ruin their appetites for the removes yet to come.

A wedding party dressed in early sixteenth-century German Landskenect costumes is a spectacular affair. PHOTO BY DICK CLARK

Between removes, there was entertainment, as well as toasts and speeches by those at the high table. Gifts were exchanged by the host and his guests, and presentations were made to the nobility by those at the lower tables as a sign of gratitude for being invited to such a fine event. The presents were customarily held up for the entire audience to see, and oohs and aahs of appreciation were an expected part of the display. At the end of the meal, there might be some form of theatrical performance, often of a religious nature, and finally, dancing to the accompaniment of court musicians. A lavish feast could go on for most of the day and well into the night. On important state occasions, rounds of feasting and reveling could stretch on for days or an entire week.

There were instances when the nobility hosted feasts for the peasants and villagers who worked on their estates. Unless the lord was unusually friendly, such largesse only took place when it was demanded by local custom or decreed by king or church. The celebration of a successful harvest, the birth of a child into the noble household, usually a firstborn male, or

the wedding of the lord's children, particularly the eldest son, all demanded some form of public revelry. On such occasions, the festivities were usually held on the grounds of the lord's estate, manor house, or castle. The amount of food provided to the populace depended entirely on the wealth and generosity of the lord. Ale and bread were basic requirements. These might be supplemented with cheese and meats, but on some occasions, the villagers were expected to supply themselves with anything beyond ale and bread.

Obviously, you'll want to recreate something more impressive than a humble peasant feast, but it is unlikely that many of us can afford to put on a celebration as grand as those hosted by the medieval kings of England and Europe. Consequently, we must look to the third major social group in medieval society, the rich merchants and minor nobility, known at the time as "the middling sort." Like many of us in the modern world, they tried hard to emulate the diet, customs, and manners of their social superiors but were constrained by a realistic budget. Consequently, they feasted on elaborate versions of foods they already knew and liked; foods they could be assured their guests would also like. Extra preparation time, a few special herbs and spices to punch up the taste, and an impressive presentational style guaranteed a warm reception at the table without the risk of overspending or producing a dish so exotic no one would eat it.

Most of the people in this class had access to a space large enough to accommodate their guests. Wealthy merchants would have rented their local guild hall, and the manor house of the petit nobility would have had a large enough dining hall to accommodate their guests. Like us, they were more likely to invite friends and business acquaintances they already liked, or wanted to get to know better, than to call in the entire village or potential military allies and their entourage. The middle class did, however, strive to emulate royalty in the order of seating and strict adherence to social protocol.

Party decorations, as we think of them, did not exist in the Middle Ages. Christmas was marked by decorating the great hall with any available evergreen plant, primarily pine, holly, and ivy, but otherwise it was a simple matter of putting out the best of every-thing you had. When important company was coming, the hosts displayed all their best pewter, silver, and, if they were really rich, gold plate. Heraldic flags and banners were hung from rafters and beams, and among those who could afford them, tapestries were hung on the walls. The idea was not only to make the house look festive, but like the celebration itself, to show off the power and wealth of the hosts.

Beyond the specific celebrations mentioned above, most medieval holidays were religious in nature. The modern word *holiday* is, in fact, a corruption of the words *Holy Day*. In addition to the requisite church attendance, major religious festivals were celebrated in much the same way as secular holidays, except among the clergy, who frequently used Holy Days as times of fasting and penance. The vast array of religious holidays that were regularly observed during the Middle Ages makes us wonder how the people got any work done at all. In practice, only the most important religious holidays were universally observed outside the monastic community. Families, villages, towns, and the nobility selected from among the rest as a means of recognizing their patron saints and days of particular personal or local significance.

CHAPTER 3

ALENDAR OF MEDIEVAL HOLIDAYS

Below is a fairly complete list of the more important medieval Holy Days and secular holidays. For saints of local significance, we have included the patron saints of England, Scotland, Wales, Ireland, Spain, and France. Other nationalities had their own patrons, as did virtually every county, town, guild, church, school, and household. You may pick your favorite as an occasion to hold your own feast or, if there is no particular theme to your celebration, pick a saint whose special day falls near the time you want to hold your feast. If you wish to hold a Christmas or Twelfth Night celebration or a medieval wedding, the next two chapters deal with customs specifically associated with those occasions.

All the calendar dates below are based on the old Julian calendar, which was in use until 1582, when the Gregorian calendar came into use. After that time, many of the religious feast days were changed, so they will not all correspond with their modern counterparts.

Scattered throughout the calendar are days marked as Ember Days. These were days of particular dedication to fasting, prayer, and beseeching God for forgiveness of sins. Ember Days take place four times a year, each time on successive Wednesdays, Fridays, and Saturdays. The first group of Ember Days occurs during the week following the first Sunday in Lent, the next is in the week after Whitsun (seven weeks after Easter), the third follows Holy Cross Day (September 14), and the last falls on the Wednesday, Friday, and Saturday following St. Lucy's Day (December 13).

JANUARY

1st. Circumcision of Christ. From the thirteenth century onward, also **New Year.** Prior to that time, the **New Year** in England began on March 25. As part of the traditional New Year's festivities, dumb shows (mummer plays where no words were spoken) were presented in churches and at feasts in great halls.

6th. Twelfth Day, or Epiphany. The twelfth day after Christmas, this was marked by a major feast held on the previous evening, known as Twelfth Night. It formally brought to an end the Christmas season.

FEBRUARY

2nd. Candlemas, or Purification of the Virgin Mary. In Ireland, the Feast of St. Bridget. Marks the day when Mary was allowed to reenter the temple after having given birth to Jesus. On this day, women traditionally processed to the local church carrying lighted candles. The traditional color for this festival was white.

14th. St. Valentine's Day. During the Middle Ages, as now, the occasion was a time of declaring one's love and praying to St. Valentine, patron saint of lovers. Local fairs were often held at this time, probably as a break from the long, dark months of winter, which were now coming to an end.

Variable. Shrove Tuesday. Falling six weeks and five days before Easter, Shrove Tuesday marked the last day before the beginning of the Lenten season. Because many people gave up meat, other favorite foods, and sex during Lent as a sign of penance (to be shriven means to be cleansed of all sin), Shrove Tuesday was often marked by feasting and revelry, even in churches

where dinner was eaten from the altar. This tradition continues today in the custom of Mardi Gras, which literally translates from the French as Fat Tuesday. The day before Shrove Tuesday, Shrove Monday, was often marked by public sporting events in which entire communities took part. While the nobles held jousting tournaments, villagers participated in games including tug-of-war (usually across an obstacle like a fence or stream), skipping contests, chasing a greased pig, marbles, climbing a greased pole, and "camping," the rules for which can be found in chapter 11. Bull and bear baiting and cock fighting were also popular entertainments now and throughout the warm months of the year. There was also a tradition that people who wished to change their fortunes would smash their pottery.

Variable. Ash Wednesday. The day after Shrove Tuesday, Ash Wednesday was the official beginning of Lent. Everyone attended mass, at which time the priest marked their foreheads with ashes in the sign of the cross. The Wednesday, Friday, and Saturday following Ash Wednesday were Ember Days, when good Christians were supposed to do particularly severe penance, giving up many foods and spending their time praying.

MARCH

1st. St. David's Day. Celebrated in Wales only, St. David's Day, commemorating the patron saint of Wales, was celebrated with church services and local celebrations. The day was marked by the wearing of a leek in the band of one's hat.

17th. St. Patrick's Day. Marked by parades and celebrations, St. Patrick's Day, commemorating the patron saint of Ireland, was the high point of secular celebration in Ireland and rivaled Christmas for general merrymaking. St. Patrick's symbol is the shamrock, which is seen as representative of the Holy Trinity.

18th. Feast of St. Edward the Confessor. In England, this was an important observance of the last completed reign of an Anglo-Saxon king prior to the Norman invasion. He was the patron saint of England from shortly after his death until the mid-thirteenth century, when he was replaced by St. George.

21st. Feast of St. Benedict. Celebrated primarily among members of the Benedictine monastic order. Benedict was widely revered throughout western Europe and England as the founder of the first monastic house.

25th. The Annunciation. Prior to the thirteenth century, the beginning of the **New Year** in England. Marked the day the angel of the Lord announced to the Virgin Mary that she would conceive Jesus. The traditional color for this festival was white.

Variable. Palm Sunday. The Sunday before Easter. Commemorated Jesus' arrival in Jerusalem, when the citizens of the town strewed palm leaves in His path. Because palms were virtually nonexistent in northern Europe and England, parishioners processed to church carrying rushes or willow wands in their hands.

Variable. Good Friday. The Friday before Easter. Marked the day of Jesus' crucifixion. The day was spent in prayer and contemplation. The traditional color for this festival was yellow, the medieval color of mourning.

Variable. Holy Saturday. The day before Easter.

Variable. Easter Sunday. Falling on the first Sunday after the first full moon on or after March 21. If the full moon is on a Sunday, the next Sunday is Easter. Easter always falls sometime between March 22 and April 25. Celebrated by Christians everywhere as the day Jesus rose from the dead, bringing the possibility of salvation from sin. The traditional color for this festival was white.

Variable. Hocktide. The Sunday after Easter, Hocktide was a time of paying the taxes, tolls, and rents and collecting debts for the first quarter of the year—therefore the name hocktide related to getting out of hock, or debt.

APRIL

1st. All Fool's, April Fool's Day. Celebrated since the second century, the custom of playing jokes and general tomfoolery may have had its roots in the mocking of Jesus by Roman soldiers and the mob in Jerusalem prior to his crucifixion. Because the weather had most likely turned fair by this time, martial sporting events were often held. Among the most popular were archery and quarterstaff contests (quarterstaffs were eight-foot-long poles that combatants used

to "break the heads" of their opponents). Other traditional observances for the feast included the fools parade, where revelers disguised themselves with costumes and masks and paraded through the town or village, demanding entrance into homes. Not even the homes of the great and powerful could be shut to the fools parade, and once inside, they would demand food and drink. This is not unlike the Halloween custom of trick or treating. All Fool's also traditionally marked the beginning of the spring planting season.

23rd. St. George's Day. Best known as the slayer of the dragon, St. George was the patron saint of soldiers everywhere and, after the displacement of St. Edward the Confessor in the thirteenth century, the patron saint of England. The traditional color for this festival was blue. Public plays were often performed to tell the story of St. George and his victory over the dragon to rescue a maiden, who had been taken prisoner by the beast.

25th. St. Mark the Evangelist.

MAY

1st. May Day. Feast of Sts. Philip and Jacob the Apostles. As the beginning of summer, May Day was a time of great celebration, most of which was held outdoors. Spring flowers were woven into garlands and wreaths, which were tied to wagons and carts and worn around the heads of unmarried women, who traditionally danced around a Maypole erected in the center of the village green. Because the young maidens had thus consented to put themselves on display, May Day became the unofficial beginning of the courting season. The first market and trade fairs were held in early May, both because the first produce was available and because local tradesmen were anxious to sell the items they had made over the long, dark winter. It was also probably the first time in months that the rough

medieval roads were passable. May Day was undoubtedly one of the most joyous and boisterous festivals of the year.

3rd. Holy Rood Day. Celebrating the discovery of the cross on which Jesus was crucified, this was primarily a religious observance.

26th. Feast of St. Augustine.

Variable. Rogation Sunday. Falling five weeks after Easter, Rogation Sunday was a time of asking God to forgive sins and to bless the land for the coming growing season. The word *rogation* means beseeching or asking. During the ceremony, parishioners would process around the boundaries of the parish, bearing a cross and banners, asking a variety of saints to intercede with God on behalf of crops, livestock, and, in fishing communities, the bounty of the sea. As a sign of their sincerity, members of the procession would distribute alms to the poor and needy. At the end of the procession, they would assemble at the parish church for mass and communion.

Variable. Ascension Day, or Holy Thursday. This Thursday marked the celebration of Christ ascending into heaven. In England, holy wells noted for their association with saints and certain healing powers were decorated, or "dressed," with flowers. Bundles of willow wands tied with blue ribbons were carried to church.

Variable. Whitsun, or White Sunday, now Pentecost. Falling ten days after Ascension Day and seven weeks after Easter Sunday. The Wednesday, Friday, and Saturday after Whitsun were Ember Days to be observed by prayer, penance, and fasting. After the solemnity of Sunday, the following week became a time of public fairs and festivals, where Morris dancing and mystery plays were performed. A special Whitsun ale was often brewed and distributed or sold. Popular games were the same as those on Shrove Tuesday. The traditional color for this festival was red.

JUNE

24th. St. John the Baptist. Based on the pagan holiday of Midsummer, this feast day was supposed to mark the birth of St. John the Baptist, Jesus' cousin, who foretold Jesus' coming. Because St. John preached in the wilderness of Judea, people in many places decorated the outside of their houses with greenery. The traditional color for this festival was white. Despite the church's attempts to stamp out all pagan traditions, the lighting of a midsummer bonfire on midsummer's eve (the evening of June 23) survived in even the most staunchly Christian communities. At this time, the fairy folk and ghosts were believed to walk abroad, and the wildflower Saint-John's-wort was picked at this time as a charm against illness and bad luck. Surprisingly, the church seems, generally, to have taken it with good grace. This was also a time of collecting summer rents and taxes.

29th. Feast of Sts. Peter and Paul the Apostles.

Variable. Trinity Sunday. Falling one week after Whitsun, Trinity was marked by contemplation of the Holy Trinity (God the Father, Son, and Holy Spirit) and the performance of miracle and mystery plays, which told the story of the Bible from the creation through the resurrection of Jesus. The traditional color for this festival was white.

Variable. Corpus Christi. Celebrated on the first Thursday after Trinity Sunday, Corpus Christi gave thanks for the sacrament of Holy Communion. The day was celebrated with public festivities, including a procession through the streets of the town, during which the host (communion wafers) was processed through the streets and religious plays were performed by local guilds and monastic houses. In Coventry, England, a fair was held in commemoration of Lady Godgifu (now known as Godiva), who rode through the town "clad only in her virtue" (stark naked) in protest of her husband, Earl Leofric, who brutalized and oppressed his subjects. The traditional color for this festival was red.

JULY

7th. Translation of St. Thomas the Martyr. A distinctly English holiday, this day marked the anniversary of moving the bones of Archbishop Thomas à Becket from their tomb to a shrine in Canterbury Cathedral, after his canonization.

15th. St. Swithin's Day. Not much observed, but it was believed that whatever the weather on this day, so it would remain for the next forty days.

22nd. St. Mary Magdalene.

25th. St. James the Apostle and St. Christopher. St. James was the patron saint of Spain, where he is known as St. Iago. His day was universally celebrated throughout the country, but nowhere were the celebrations any larger or more devout than in Campostella, where the shrine of St. James is the heart of the cathedral and the culmination point of one of Christendom's most popular pilgrimages. St. Christopher was the patron saint of travelers, and his feast date was particularly observed by those who were about to undertake a long journey or who traveled habitually in the course of their work.

Variable. July was the traditional time for the beginning of religious pilgrimages, and consequently, many outdoor religious services were held.

AUGUST

1st. Feast of St. Peter in Chains (in Latin, St. Peter ad Vincula). In commemoration of the miracles performed by the chains that bound St. Peter, while he was imprisoned in Rome awaiting crucifixion. This was also Lammas Day (possibly derived from "Loaf Mass"), the time when thanks was given for a successful wheat harvest.

5th. St. Dominic. Primarily observed by members of the Dominican monastic order in honor of their founder.

10th. St. Lawrence the Martyr.

15th. Assumption of Our Lady. Marked the day when the Virgin Mary was carried into heaven. This was an essentially religious holiday, but there were occasional parades, particularly where the local church or monastery was dedicated to Our Lady.

24th. St. Bartholomew.

25th. St. Louis IX. Patron saint of France. Formerly King Louis IX of France. Although he did not die until 1270, by 1297 he had already been canonized and almost instantly became France's most popular saint.

28th. St. Augustine of Hipo. Celebrated primarily among members of the Augustinian monastic order in honor of their patron.

SEPTEMBER

8th. Nativity of Our Lady. Ostensibly celebrating the Virgin Mary's birthday, this was traditionally celebrated as a harvest festival. Harvesting was always

blessed by the church, partly as a display of God's blessing on the harvest, and partly because, by canon law, the church received one-tenth of the entire harvest. The final cartload of grain to be brought in from the field was followed in procession and accompanied by much singing and ceremony. At the feast that signaled the end of the harvest in almost every rural community, the tables were decorated with dolls made from wheat shafts, the dolls being burned after the feast was over. As the field workers blew off steam with reveling and drinking, harvest festivals obtained a reputation for being excessively rowdy. Although this was a patently pagan custom, the church turned a blind eye.

14th. Exaltation of the Cross. A Holy Rood day. Supposedly the date of the discovery of the "true cross," this day was traditionally celebrated as a part of the harvest season festivities. The following Wednesday, Friday, and Saturday were Ember Days, observed with fasting, prayer, and penance. The traditional color for this festival was red.

21st. St. Matthew the Apostle.

29th. Michaelmas, or Feast of St. Michael the Archangel. Important to both church and laity, this feast signaled the end of the harvest and of the agricultural year. It was also the day when the last rents of the year were traditionally collected, tithes were due, and accounts were settled. It was a time of great public celebration and feasting to mark the harvest. One of

the most unique elements of this occasion was the appearance of "horn dancers," a troupe of men wearing or carrying sets of deer antlers, who danced in public marketplaces to the accompaniment of drums and pipes. The tradition may date back to an ancient pagan custom celebrating the hunt.

OCTOBER

9th. St. Denys' Day. Patron saint of the city of Paris. St. Denys' Day was celebrated throughout France, but primarily in the capital, both with church services and with parades and festivals.

18th. St. Luke the Evangelist.

25th. St. Crispin's Day. Primarily remembered as the anniversary of the battle of Agincourt (1415), when England's King Henry V put the entire combined French army and cavalry to rout with a band of only seven thousand men. Thereafter, it was celebrated in England as a day of military victory. We can assume the French chose to ignore the occasion entirely.

28th. Sts. Simon and Jude the Apostles.

31st. All Hallows' Eve. A time of spiritual unrest, when the souls of the dead, along with ghosts and evil spirits, were believed to walk the land. Church bells were rung and fires lit to guide them on their way and deflect them from haunting honest Christian folk. Barns and homes were blessed to protect people

and livestock from the effects of witches, who were believed to accompany the malignant spirits as they traveled the earth. Although it was a time for divination, casting spells, and telling ghost stories in rural communities, woe to anyone denounced to the church for doing so. This may seem like innocent fun today, but it was deadly serious stuff during the Middle Ages.

NOVEMBER

1st. All Hallows' Day, or All Saints' Day. The word *hallow* was simply another word for saint. The feast was dedicated to all the truly holy people in the history of Christianity. The traditional color for this festival was white.

2nd. All Souls' Day. A time when prayers were said for the souls of the dead and penance done to help extricate the dead from purgatory.

20th. St. Edmund the King and Martyr. Again, a uniquely English celebration. St. Edmund had been the ninth-century king of Norfolk, then an independent kingdom of Anglo-Saxon England. He was martyred by the Danes in 870.

25th St. Catherine's Day. Famous for surviving torture on a spiked wheel (the Catherine wheel), only to be beheaded, St. Catherine was the most popular female saint of the Middle Ages, venerated by both men and women. Many guilds, churches, ships, and organizations were dedicated to her name. On her festival, great processions were held in her honor.

Variable. Advent. Beginning the fourth Sunday before Christmas, Advent lasted through Christmas Eve. Missing Sunday services during this period would be unthinkable.

DECEMBER

6th. St. Nicholas' Day. Precursor to the Santa Claus tradition, the feast of St. Nicholas was observed by the presentation of gifts to children, accompanied by family-oriented merrymaking. Traditionally, the feast of St. Nicholas began more than a month of celebrations, worship services, and feasts surrounding the Christmas season. In cathedrals throughout England and Europe, "boy bishops" were elected in commemoration of St. Nicholas' compassion for children. From St. Nicholas' Day until the Feast of the Holy Innocents (December 28), the mock bishops were allowed to undertake all ecclesiastical duties except delivering the mass.

8th. The Conception of Our Lady. Celebrating St. Anne becoming pregnant with the future Virgin Mary.

11th. St. Andrew's Day. Andrew is the patron saint of Scotland, where his celebration was widely observed with both religious services and traditional

Scottish games such as the caber toss, throwing the stone, and displays of martial prowess.

13th. St. Lucy's Day. Noted here as a reminder that the next Wednesday, Friday, and Saturday are Ember Days.

21st. St. Thomas the Apostle.

25th. Christmas. The most joyous time of the year, Christmas marked the birth of Jesus. The season was celebrated with feasts, dancing, wassailing through the streets, and religious and secular plays, all set amid garlands of holly and evergreen.

26th. St. Stephen's Day. St. Stephen is considered the first Christian martyr.

28th. Feast of the Holy Innocents. Commemorating King Herod's slaughter of thousands of children in an attempt to kill the infant Jesus, this was a day of particular importance for pregnant women, families with sick children, and mothers who had lost children through disease, accident, or stillbirth, which included almost every family during the Middle Ages.

29th. Feast of St. Thomas the Archbishop and Martyr. This day celebrated the life and work of Thomas à Becket, archbishop of Canterbury, murdered on this date in 1169 on the order of King Henry II.

Only four years after his martyrdom, Becket was canonized. His shrine in Canterbury Cathedral, Canterbury, England, became a place of pilgrimage for people throughout Europe, only succeeded in popularity by St. Peters in Rome and St. James in Compostella, Spain. The celebration of his feast day, however, was most popular among the English people.

CHAPTER 4

# CHRISTMAS CELEBRATIONS

Long before Europeans began recording their history, they celebrated a great winter festival. There were perfectly practical reasons for having one last, great feast before the onset of the most severe weather. All the carefully preserved stocks of salted meats, dried fish, grain, and milled flour had been put aside, and any remaining provisions needed to be consumed before they went bad. In this primitive world, the privations of winter were a real threat to survival, and as an act of defiance against this long, dark season, people chose to celebrate. The human spirit was determined to live on till the next growing season, and to do so with bravery and good cheer.

But the winter festivals of pre-Christian Europe were far more than railing against the storm and snow that came with the final season of the year. A major element of the old pagan winter festivals was dramatizing the death of the old year and celebrating the beginning of a new one. These celebrations had a distinctly religious aspect, because they were an affirmation of man's relationship with nature and an attempt to appease the gods who controlled it. At the time of year when the sun appeared to decline in the sky, and deprivation threatened the very survival of the community, winter festivals were an attempt to appease whatever mysterious forces were responsible for bringing about the bleakness of the season and to encourage the return of the sun and the fertility of the land. This aspect of the festivals was connected to standard pagan fertility rites. The food consumed at the feasts was simultaneously a celebration and a sacrifice to the unknown gods of nature. In attempting to drive away the darkness of winter, lights and fires were important to these festivals; the fire attracted, or called out to,

the sun to hasten its return. Similarly, the use of evergreens to decorate homes was far more than an attractive adornment. Because these were the only things that remained green when all else was dead and brown, they were symbolic of the continuity of life. Another factor in the popularity of midwinter celebrations was that rural communities, which made up over 95 percent of the population of the ancient world, had plenty of spare time during this season and needed some sort of festival to cheer them up. Farmers had little to do during the winter apart from milking and feeding the cows and tending the other livestock. The plow and other implements of cultivation had been put away until spring.

There were two distinct lines of winter holiday festivities in the ancient world: those of Romanized southern Europe, and those associated with the Yule celebrations of the Germanic north. The later Roman Empire had three important midwinter festivals: Saturnalia, which began on December 17; the Kalends, on January 1; and the Birthday of the Unconquered Sun, on December 25. Saturnalia was named for the early Roman god Saturnus, whose name meant "plenty" or "bounty," and his festival was characterized by revelry, feasting, and drunkenness. During Saturnalia and the Kalends, which inaugurated the new year and gave us the word *calendar*, buildings were brightly lit and decorated with evergreens, while holiday processions crowded the streets and families exchanged presents. Public and private feasts were presided over by a mock ruler, or a master of revels, and the normal social order was turned on its head: Masters waited on their servants; pastimes like gambling, which were forbidden at other times, were permitted; and men dressed as women or in animal skins, while the women dressed in men's clothes. There was even a special place in the Roman festival season for children, celebrated as the feast of Juvinalia.

In the midst of these weeks of revelry came a day set aside for the celebration of the sun, whose annual crisis at the winter solstice formed the heart of almost all ancient winter festivals. It was the occasion when the sun appeared, from the perspective of northern Europe, to stand low and still on the southern horizon before rising with the passing days in anticipation of spring. With the passing of the solstice, the sun stopped receding and began returning northward toward the zenith. The sun briefly standing still was a noteworthy event for a heavenly body that was deified in many religions. Some early religious ceremonies were designed to ensure, by magic and sacrifice, that this would happen. Although celebrated throughout the Roman world, the Day of the Birth of the Unconquered Sun, or Sol Invictus, was in particular the great feast day of Mithraism, a salvationist religion popular among soldiers in the Roman world, and a vigorous competitor with early Christianity. By the time Christianity became an established religion in the fourth century A.D., the winter solstice had been fixed on December 25.

The northern European festival of Yuletide had many similarities to its counterparts in the Roman Empire. There was the same gargantuan feasting, and the drinking and carousing of the Germanic tribes were as copious and boisterous as the revelry of the Romans. The emphasis on the lighting of great bonfires was both a ritual encouragement to the waning sun and a bringer of festive cheer in the dead of winter. There was a peculiar northern European preoccupation with the dark forces of the night during Yuletide. Ghosts and demons were believed to roam freely through the vast forests of northern Europe on long, dark winter nights. In Scandinavia, Julebuk appeared in a devilish mask and horns, but strangely, he also brought gifts to children. In parts of Germany, legends of a similar hideous monster lived on into modern times as Klausauf, a companion to St. Nicholas in his seasonal visit to children. It is from the Germanic Yuletide celebrations that many of the traditions of our modern Christmas come: the warmth and good cheer around the Yule log, while outside there is darkness, cold, and "things that go bump in the night."

Early Christians did not celebrate the birth of Christ. The celebration of birthdays had long tradi-

tions in the pagan world, and the Gospels say nothing about the actual date of Christ's birth. Possibly, because it was widely believed that Christ would return in the very near future, the exact date of His birth seemed unimportant. As Christianity developed, the concept of Jesus as both fully divine and also fully human became accepted dogma. With the acceptance of Jesus as God in human form, there was an urgent desire to celebrate the occasion of His nativity. Jesus had to have an official birthday. The need to celebrate Jesus' birth, the traditional pagan rites of the winter solstice, and other elements, including Saturnalia, all converged by the fourth century A.D. to fix the Christian Feast of the Nativity on December 25. Christmas is, in fact, a classic example of the Christian Church coming to terms with the traditional customs and rites of the people, superimposing a Christian festival on a pagan holiday.

In Anglo-Saxon England, the Christian festival dovetailed easily into existing pagan practices, for December 25 was both the beginning of the Anglo-Saxon year and the time of the Yule festivities. Recognizing that people were not easily weaned from their traditions, Pope Gregory the Great (540–604) became an enthusiastic advocate of converting pagans to Christianity by coming to terms with existing social and religious customs. He wrote to St. Augustine of Canterbury when the latter was embarking on his mission to England in 596, telling him how the old festivities of the "killing time" could be used by Christianity:

> Nor let them now sacrifice animals to the Devil, but to the praise of God kill animals for their own eating, and render thanks to the Giver of all things for their abundance; so that while some outward joys are retained for them, they may the more easily respond to inward joys. For from obdurate minds it is undoubtedly impossible to cut off everything at once, because he who strives to ascend to the highest places rises by degrees or steps and not by leaps.

Despite Pope Gregory's hopes, the pagan elements in the Anglo-Saxon midwinter feast probably remained stronger for the majority of early Anglo-Saxon Christians than the religious aspects. The Viking invasions of England in the eighth and ninth centuries reinvigorated pagan traditions, while Christian priests were scarce and often as illiterate as their flocks. Away from the influence of prelates and monasteries, it is likely that the Yuletide tradition remained

strong and the midwinter feast throughout northern Europe remained substantially what it had been before the coming of Christianity, a time of heavy drinking and carousing among blazing Yule logs in buildings adorned with evergreens. Many of the customs accompanying the festivities—the mummers' plays, whose usual theme was a dramatic presentation of death and resurrection, the wassailing (blessing) of fruit trees by pouring ale on them, and even the games that have become our blind man's buff and leapfrog—were, consciously or unconsciously, derived from fertility rites.

From the beginning of its celebration, we find an ambiguity in the attitude of fervent Christians to the festive season. There is an emphasis on the fact that it is Christian and, along with Easter, the most impor-

tant of festivals. There is, at the same time, an uneasy feeling that many aspects of the celebration are all too worldly.

Early Christians were warned against "feasting to excess, dancing and crowning the doors [with evergreens]" and urged to keep "the celebration of the festival after an heavenly and not after an earthly manner." That the "true spirit of Christmas" and the central miracle of the Christian religion—God becoming man—were constantly in danger of being lost amidst the revelry of Saturnalia, or Yuletide, has been feared since Christianity first chose to celebrate the birth of its Savior. Many a priest, prelate, and minister has preached to his congregation in similar vein, from 389 A.D. to the present day.

THE MEDIEVAL CHRISTMAS CELEBRATION

During the Middle Ages, Christmas was observed in a variety of ways. Our word *Christmas*, which seems first to have been used in Britain on the eve of the Norman Conquest, is derived from the Middle English term for "Christ's Mass." Central to the celebration of the Nativity was the mass, which had been established by the year 600 and did not notably change throughout the Middle Ages (a complete twelfth-century Latin mass is found at the end of the next chapter). In medieval England there were, in fact, three masses celebrated on Christmas Day. The first and most characteristic was at midnight, the Angel's Mass, taking the vein that the light of salvation appeared at the darkest moment of the darkest date in the very depth of winter. The second, the Shepherd's Mass, came at dawn, and the third, the Mass of the Divine Word, during the day.

The season of Advent, the forty days leading up to Christmas, was being observed in the Western Church by the year 500 A.D. Although St. Nicholas was a very popular medieval saint, and his feast day came in Advent, on December 6, he did not play his part in Christmas as Father Christmas or Santa Claus until after the Reformation. But it is significant to note that the forty days of Advent combined with the twelve days of Christmas, or in some cases, the forty days between Christmas and Candlemas, were a time of great celebration. Why hold parties that might last up to three months? There are many good reasons, not the least of which had to do with the fact that travel was difficult and dangerous. It might take guests and relatives weeks to gather, and they were unlikely to undertake such an arduous journey for a simple evening meal.

Despite the best and most creative endeavors of the church, the essentially secular nature of Christmas persisted and endured through the Middle Ages and into the modern age. The Twelve Days of Christmas were the main national holiday in medieval England and were popularly observed as a time for feasting, dancing, singing, sporting, gambling, and general excess and indulgence. Part of the cause for celebration undoubtedly arises from the security that comes with winter. True, the weather could be harsh and cruel, and food and stores could be in short supply, but political enemies were unlikely to start a war or undertake a siege under such conditions. One is alive, safe from enemy threat, surrounded by friends and good company, and has enjoyed plentiful harvests and good hunting with which to cover the tables and fill the belly . . . by all means, celebrate.

Throughout the Middle Ages, the festival remained, despite the church's best efforts, obstinately worldly. To some extent, Christmas can be seen as a contest between the dictates of the church and the popular culture of the people. Ecclesiastical opinion viewed the sensual enjoyment of Christmas festivities as either a necessary indulgence of the weak and fallible or a dangerous distraction from Christian worship. Medieval royalty and nobility, on the other hand, competed with each other in their displays of grand celebration at the Christmas season.

The feast hosted by King John of England at Christmas 1213 is supposed to have surpassed the most sumptuous and gargantuan banquets of any previous time, but the celebrations of his son Henry III were on an even grander scale. In 1252, he entertained a thousand knights and peers at York; the feast was so expensive that the archbishop of York alone gave six hundred fat oxen and £2,700 toward the feasting. A century and a half later, Richard II provided two thousand oxen and two hundred barrels of wine for the ten thousand who dined daily at his expense. It was incumbent upon kings, barons, and lesser magnates to dispense hospitality and provide good cheer to the greatest extent their resources would allow. Staging a magnificent feast was tantamount to mounting an army in the field. It was a display of wealth and power. After all, who but a great king could find, and afford, several thousand oxen to serve his dinner guests?

These public displays of wealth, generosity, and Christmas cheer were more than simple vanity; they were good politics. They enhanced the reputation of hosts, could bind together alliances and strengthen feudal bonds, and were probably essential to the survival of poor retainers and peasants during the bleakest time of the year. The size of the banquets obviously varied in sumptuousness according to the resources of the celebrants. The menu was varied, with soups and stews, birds and fish, breads and puddings, but a common element was the Yule boar—the entire beast for those who could afford it, just the head served as a decoration for the high table, or in more humble households, a meat pie shaped like a boar.

Churches, castle feast halls, public buildings, and houses were all decorated with ivy, mistletoe, holly, and anything that remained green. These decorations were put up during Advent and remained in place until the eve of Candlemas. Gift giving took place on New Year, unconsciously continuing a pagan tradition of Roman origin. The tradition of the Christmas present was not part of the medieval Christmas, although presents were given to children on December 6, St. Nicholas' Day. The types of entertainment people might employ to keep from getting bored are succinctly summarized in a letter written by Margaret Paston on Christmas Eve 1459, after she had inquired how her Norfolk neighbor, Lady Morley, had conducted her household, which had been in mourning the previous Christmas just after Lady Morley had been widowed: "There were no disguisings [acting], nor harping, luting or singing, nor any lewd sports, but just playing at the tables [backgammon] and chess and cards. Such sports she gave her folk leave to play and no other."

Mention of disguisings calls to our attention the Christmas plays that were a part of late medieval entertainment throughout Britain and Europe (the complete text of a typical holiday play is found in chapter 12). Mention by Lady Morley of "lewd sports" is probably a reference to the carol dance. The leader of the dance sang a verse of the carol, and a ring of dancers responded with the chorus. Carol dances were often suggestive of their pagan ancestors, where, for instance, holly and ivy had fertility associations with male and female. Further music for the celebration of the season was provided by hymns, sung in Latin or French.

Another important aspect of medieval Christmas festivities was that they provided a release from the normal social rules and allowed authority to be symbolically overturned. The old Saturnalia customs of cross-dressing in the clothes of the opposite sex or putting on the skins of animals continued to be associated with Christmas, as did gambling and the practice of role reversal, where superiors waited on those of inferior rank, which survives to this day in the British Army. The reign of "Lords of Misrule" in castle feast halls and the elections of "Boy Bishops" in cathedrals are both customs that appear to have become popular in the thirteenth century.

Perhaps it was a combination of viewing Jesus as an infant, the role-switching aspects of Roman Saturnalia, and the association of St. Nicholas with children that gave rise to the curiously widespread medieval custom of appointing a boy to the position of bishop for the Christmas period. St. Nicholas, whose feast day falls on December 6, was bishop of Myra, in modern

Turkey. Among Nicholas' roles was patron saint of children. The unsavory story that tied Nicholas to children claims that during a time of famine, an innkeeper, short on food, killed three schoolboys, pickled their flesh, and stored it in a barrel. When Bishop Nicholas happened by, he restored the three boys to life. In medieval representations of St. Nicholas, the saint is often portrayed standing next to a cask from which three boys are emerging.

Boy Bishops were found in England by the first quarter of the thirteenth century, and the custom was not finally abolished until 1559. At Salisbury Cathedral, to select a specific case, the Boy Bishop was chosen by cathedral choristers from among their number on St. Nicholas' Day and performed his pseudo-episcopal office, which included everything except delivering the mass, for just over three weeks, until the night of the Feast of the Holy Innocents.

Following his election and investiture, the Boy Bishop, like a true bishop, would set out with his attendants on a visitation throughout his bishopric, imposing correct doctrine and discipline as he traveled. The visitation of the Boy Bishop and his retinue to ecclesiastical establishments and noble households in the vicinity might last several weeks and involve being given many gifts and treated to lavish entertainments. Many of the gifts would later be sold to cover expenses. The whole carnival of the Boy Bishop was splendid entertainment, sometimes irreverent and unruly, but it suited its era by allowing ritual protest against the rigid authority structure that was integral to maintaining social order. This peculiar custom, and that of the Lord of Misrule, were medieval incarnations of the older, pagan customs of the "king of the bean" and the "yule lord" who would receive supreme power and authority for the season, after which he would be ritually sacrificed. The Lord of Misrule was simply a random member of the populace who was somehow selected to serve as Lord or King for the duration of the festivities. As such, he presented a serious upheaval to an otherwise stagnant social order.

The medieval church made a serious attempt both to ensure that the more pagan and popular aspects of Christmas were firmly harnessed within the religious aspects of the Christmas festival, and to popularize specifically Christian aspects of winter celebrations. Old customs could always be reinterpreted by the Church, but most important was telling of the story of Christ's birth in terms accessible to the common people.

Nativity plays began in medieval churches, as seasonal embellishments to the liturgy, and eventually passed from churches to the streets and from the clergy to the laity, losing the Latin dialogue in the process. But the commoners had their own plays, and these were of pagan origin. These annual performances, known as mumming plays, are probably the oldest surviving feature of the Christmas festivities and put all the rest into proper perspective. They present, in dramatic form, the contest between the powers of light and darkness. The basic plot is always the same, but the details have often become blurred.

In most instances, the plays were not written down until very recent times. Players learned their parts from their elders, who had, in turn, learned them from their fathers and grandfathers. Each actor had to play the role exactly as he had been taught, whether it seemed to make sense or not. Often, however, the hearing or memory of the student or teacher was faulty. In other instances, time alone can be seen as having altered the characters that appear in the story.

The hero is usually St. George. His association with England dates from the Crusades. But in later versions, he becomes both Robyn Hode (as he is in the version of the story presented in this book) and King George. The later change may have occurred as late as the beginning of the eighteenth century, when the Georges came to the British throne. Occasionally the hero bears what was perhaps his earlier name of Bold Slasher or Bold Soldier. In some versions of the play, he is known as the Ball Roomer; almost certainly he was originally the Bold Roamer. In many of the plays, the powers of darkness are represented by the Turkish Knight (sometimes by two Turkish knights). The identification of the villain with the national enemy, the Saracens or Turks, probably dates from the time of the Crusades. But in several versions, the Turkish Knight has become the Turkey Snipe.

No matter what names the characters are given, the story remains the same. The powers of darkness fight with the hero and give him a mortal wound. As he lies dying, a frantic call goes up for the Doctor, who comes in and heals the expiring hero with his magic medicine. The dark figures steal away, and the hero rises renewed and triumphant. In some versions, the plot has become so confused that it is difficult to tell which are the good guys and which the baddies. But always somebody is brought back to life from apparently certain death.

Another frequent character is usually called Little Johnny Jack. He is a rather pathetic figure, hung with ten or a dozen cloth dolls, who represent his numerous children. Little Johnny Jack is important, for he explains how the mumming plays have managed to survive. He is unashamedly a beggar. Entering toward the end of the play, he recites a speech that reveals the mumming plays for what they became: a means by which the poor obtained Christmas charity from the rich. It was the custom for village mummers to make the rounds of the great houses in the district and perform their play in the hall, or drawing room. At each they would collect gifts of cash or food. In the Robyn Hode version of the play presented in this book, it is Friar Tuck who collects money from the audience. Since household clergy always collected offerings for the poor, this was a perfectly reasonable theatrical device. Considering the lucrative pickings available in castles and great houses around Christmastime, it is hardly surprising that the rural poor kept the plays alive for so many centuries.

One of the better-known features of the medieval Christmas celebration is the tradition of wassailing. The wassail pot was a large bowl, traditionally made of maple wood though in special circumstances of silver, filled with a mixture of warming drinks. Ale or cider, often heated, was the chief ingredient, to which were added spices, sugar, raisins, roasted apples, sliced oranges, and any other pleasant ingredients available. It was, in fact, an early kind of punch. Wassail bowls were passed around at private parties and taken around villages by singers who asked for alms. The wassailing season was from Christmas Eve to Twelfth Night, culminating in the wassailing of the apple trees—a blessing bestowed by pouring a little of the wassail onto the roots of the trees to ensure a good harvest in the coming year, a distinctly pagan holdover.

To a large extent, carol singing has replaced wassailing. The object is the same, to collect money, and the carol singers range from small children who stumble through one verse and then knock at the door, to efficiently organized parties from the local church choir who trundle around a harmonium and perform for shut-ins, the elderly, and charities. Carols were not originally confined to Christmas as they now are; there were, for instance, Easter carols, some of which may be found in modern church hymnals. Carols were also sung at the Feast of All Saints, also known as All Hallows'. When All Hallows' became secularized and popularized as Halloween, the tradition of going from door to door begging for gifts survived, but adults were replaced by children, and singing was lost in favor of calling out "trick or treat."

The carol itself originated in popular French dance songs, condemned by the church as lustful and pagan. Originally associated with Christmas only by the season in which it was sung, the carol eventually evolved into a form that was primarily religious and was therefore acceptable to the church. While carols became specifically religious in nature, they remained quite commonplace in subject, as with this fourteenth-century English example:

> Iesu, swete sone dere!
> On porful bed list thou here,
> And that me greveth sore;
> For thi cradel is ase a bere,
> Oxe and asse beth thi fere;
> Weepe ich mai tharfore.

> *Translation:*
> Sweet, dear baby Jesus,
> Your bed is so poor,
> And I grieve for you;
> Because your cradle is in a cow barn,
> The oxen and asses are your
>   companions;
> Therefore, I weep for you.

The rural poor were profoundly affected by the concept of a prince born in poverty, who was attended by shepherds and surrounded by beasts that miraculously fell on their knees before him. In the Middle Ages, country folk firmly believed that on Christmas Eve, bees sang in their hives and oxen knelt in their stalls, their heads bowed toward Jerusalem in the east.

As well known as the wassail bowl and carol is the Yule log. A Yule log once burned on every hearth at Christmas. The log was not brought into the house until Christmas Eve, and once lit, the fire was not allowed to go out until the log was entirely consumed. It had associations with the Christmas candle, which was also a common feature of Christmas festivities. Both log and candle were lit at the same moment. Placed on the table at the beginning of the feast, the Christmas candle was not to be moved, blown out, or snuffed out during the meal.

Prince Albert, the husband of Queen Victoria, is usually given the credit for introducing Christmas trees to England in 1847, from his native Germany. Certainly from that time their popularity increased rapidly, but there are records of such trees in London streets in the Middle Ages. In fact, the idea behind the Christmas tree is the same as the idea behind the Yule log and candle: It is a symbolic celebration of man's triumph over darkness and his mastery of fire.

Most cultures and religions have a myth about the theft of fire from the gods, and the legendary flaming tree has ancient, even prehistoric, origins, from Loki, to Prometheus, to the burning bush of the Bible. It is an odd ritual that we now perform, cutting down an evergreen, bringing it into our home, and decorating it with lights as though it were on fire, but it makes us somehow more comfortable. It is a tradition that reaches back to a time long before our medieval ancestors. Although there are no records of Christmas trees being lit in great halls, the halls decked with boughs of holly and pine brought color and fragrance to the dreary interiors, while the Yule log and candles provided warmth and light to vanquish the cold and dark.

Mistletoe, because of its pagan associations, was forbidden in most churches, with the notable exception of York Minster Cathedral in York, England. Mistletoe featured prominently in Norse mythology, as the plant by which the hero Baldur was slain. It was also sacred to the old Celtic religion and was cut with much ceremony by the Druids. The practice of kissing under the mistletoe is very old, and in countries where mistletoe was scarce, there was a tradition of making a kissing bush of other evergreens and decorations, to be suspended from the ceiling.

Holly has usually been a permitted Christmas decoration, although in ancient times it was considered to be the home of woodland spirits and is even today occasionally regarded as a witches' tree, and the belief that it is unlucky to bring holly into the house before Christmas Eve still survives. Ivy is likewise an accepted evergreen. On the Isle of Man, sweet cicely, which the Manx called myrrh, was said to blossom for one hour on Christmas Eve. On Christmas Day, the great thorn tree at Glastonbury Abbey in Somerset, England, bursts into flower, though some years it waits until the original Christmas Day, January 5. In either case, there is no doubt that it does flower in midwinter, something no thorn bush should do under any circumstances.

Religion as well as custom can be credited with the extravagant celebrations associated with the

Christmas season, but the basic morality of Christmas was that people should be merry and hospitable; if they were also inclined to be prayerful, all the better. Every race and code of beliefs indigenous to Europe have contributed to modern Christmas customs. The mumming plays belong to a remote and certainly pagan era. Father Christmas's sleigh, drawn through the skies by reindeer, evolved from Odin's chariot. Odin, or Wotan, the Nordic-Germanic god of war, was believed to hurtle across the night sky during the winter festival, bearing gifts for his faithful followers. When Odin and his kind were banished by Christian rulers, his place was taken by St. Nicholas. The exchange of presents is most likely a holdover from the gifts exchanged by the Romans on Kalends. The generosity of the gift exchange was reinterpreted under Christian doctrine to be a reenactment of the gifts of gold, frankincense, and myrrh brought to the baby Jesus by the wise men. Decorations of holly, mistletoe, and ivy are borrowed from Celtic and Nordic tribes. Wassailing has been inherited from ancient fertility rites, and carol singing started as little more than institutionalized begging.

For all the rules and regulations that bound medieval society, there was no absolute standard about when the Christmas season was to end. Most people ended the revelries with Epiphany, popularly known in the Middle Ages as Twelfth Night (hence the twelve days of Christmas), but many carried it through February 2, the Feast of the Purification of the Virgin, popularly known as Candlemas. In one of the most elaborate processions of the year, all parishioners processed to mass carrying a penny and a candle, both of which were offered to the priest as part of the parochial dues of the faithful. The candles were blessed and taken away to be used for such things as giving comfort during thunderstorms or to the sick and the dying. Such candles were thus important for giving people a light of solace in the face of hostile forces and stressful events. Candlemas was a closure for the long season, commencing with Advent, that drew medieval Christians to concentrate on the miraculous birth of Christ, bringing with Him the promise of salvation, while leaving at the same time space for fun, feasting, and socializing.

Medieval feast hall as it would have appeared around 1400. FROM BARLEY HALL, YORK, ENGLAND

A recreated medieval event. A nineteenth-century church assembly hall, decorated with painted banners and peopled with guests in home-made medieval costumes, makes a convincingly medieval setting.

Medieval costumes, brightly colored banners, and a few tents painted with medieval designs, and a medieval event takes on a life of its own.

A local medieval group might be willing to put on a demonstration of medieval fighting skills at your event—a performance that can lend a frightening air of authenticity to the festivities.

Costumes can be taken to any extent of authenticity you desire. Here, the authors appear as Leonardo Da Vinci and Pope Julius II at a medieval event held in 1992.

Hired entertainers, like this fire-eater, can make even a modest event something that will be talked about for years to come. PHOTO BY DICK CLARK

A mixed party of costumed and uncostumed revelers enjoy a medieval day in a park. Outdoor settings work for all time periods and remove the necessity for constructing elaborate decorations or finding an architecturally appropriate space. PHOTO BY DICK CLARK

The church may not be medieval, but the iron chandeliers and Gothic arched windows provide an evocative setting for this recreated medieval wedding. Note that the company includes guests in both medieval and modern clothes. PHOTO BY BRIAN EDWARDS; COURTESY OF SEAN AND INGRID CLOUTER

OPPOSITE: *Medieval costumes and flickering candlelight transform an otherwise ordinary evening into a romantic spectacle.*

PHOTO BY PETER SAMWORTH

A variety of costumes, candles, tankards, and wooden bowls, and guests can be magically transported 700 years into the past. PHOTO BY STEVE LUND

Arms and Banner Designs.
These coats of arms can be adapted for use as banners to decorate your feast hall. All of these designs are original medieval coats of arms from England, Ireland, and Germany. The color schemes have been changed out of respect for the families who hold the rights to these arms. You can change the designs and colors to suit your personal taste.

CHAPTER 5

EDDINGS

arriage as we have come to understand it is essentially an invention of the Middle Ages. Until well after the end of the first millennium, marriage was an entirely secular rite. Prior to 1100 A.D., most marriages had no religious ceremony connected to them. If the church was involved at all, it was only because a priest had been invited to witness the ceremony as a reliable member of the community who could verify, in writing if necessary, that the marriage had taken place. In rural communities and among the urban poor of this period, there were almost no formalized marriage rituals of any sort. The public exchange of a kiss and the announcement that a couple were married, followed by the act of consummation, were enough to satisfy the community of the legitimacy of the marriage. If a formal ceremony did take place, it was more likely to have been celebrated by the couple joining hands over the anvil of the local blacksmith and swearing their good intentions than it was to take place in a church.

It was not until the Fourth Lateran Council, in 1215, that the church included marriage in its list of holy sacraments. Once marriage became an official rite of the church, prelates everywhere were quick to encourage people to legitimize their marriage with a religious ceremony. In 1220, Bishop Richard de Marisco of Durham, England, declared:

> We enjoin that marriages be celebrated decently, with reverence, not with laughter and ribaldry, not in taverns or at public drinkings and feastings. Let no man place a ring made of rushes or of any worthless or precious material on the hand of a woman in

jest that he may more easily gain her favours, lest in thinking to jest the bond of marriage. Henceforth let no pledge of contracting marriage be given save in the presence of a priest and of three or four respectable persons summoned for the purpose.

This is not meant to indicate that marriage was taken lightly before it became a sacrament of the church. There were still rules that had to be followed. The couple had to have reached the legal age of consent: twelve for girls and fourteen for boys. Under no circumstances could women be forced to marry against their wishes and still be bound to uphold the marriage contract, at least not legally. And there was always the consideration of improving one or both families' social position through marriage. Even in relatively poor rural communities, both families tried to ensure that their children's marriage would be advantageous for all concerned. To a large extent, this meant that marriages were arranged. Parents, grandparents, elder siblings, village elders, and even the groom might all be involved in the prenuptial negotiations. The bride was almost universally excluded from determining her future husband. She did, however, have the legal right to refuse to marry anyone who did not suit her, and could appeal to both the church and civil authorities to be saved from a bad marriage proposal. The church, in particular, was very unhappy about young girls being taken advantage of by being forced to marry elderly men.

Once a match was arranged, negotiators got down to the important details: the settlement of a proper dowry. Contrary to popular belief, both sides had to contribute to the dowry, not just the bride. The size and value of the dowry were determined by the social position and wealth of the marrying parties. Assuming that both of the betrothed were of comfortable, merchant-class status, the bride's dowry might include real property such as money, gold, plate, horses, possibly some land, and even her clothes. These all became the uncontested property of the groom once the marriage had taken place. For his part, the groom had to promise that his wife would be taken care of should he precede her in death. He would guarantee that she would receive a certain portion of his income, usually between a third and a half, as long as she lived. When she died or, in many cases, if she married again, the property reverted to the groom's family. There were sometimes clauses in dowry contracts demanding that the dowries be returned if the bride died within a specified period after the wedding, usually one or two years. As long as the bride survived her first pregnancy or two and did not contract the plague, it was a good arrangement for the groom and his family.

Once the dowry was agreed upon, the betrothal was announced. This announcement, known as "publishing the bans," was, in many senses, the most important part of the medieval wedding. Bans were published several months prior to the date of the wedding. This advance notice gave time for anyone with a legitimate objection to the marriage to come forward and present his or her case. Once the bans had been published, the families of the newly engaged couple hosted a feast that rivaled the actual wedding feast. As a symbol of his honorable intentions, the groom presented the bride with a ring, traditionally engraved with both of their names. This was, essentially, an engagement ring. The bride presented the groom with a sleeve from one of her garments, one of her stockings, or both. This may seem a strange custom today, but in the Middle Ages, these "favors" were considered honored gifts. A heraldic device known as a maunch is a stylized form of a woman's sleeve. Certainly these portions of clothing suggested that the groom was getting closer to undressing his new bride. Just as certainly, he didn't have long to wait for the real thing.

Many medieval betrothal feasts ended by the happy couple being sent off to bed to begin a cohabitation that often lasted right through the wedding itself. Living together as man and wife during the betrothal period enabled a prospective groom time to ensure that his wife-to-be was not barren. As long as she was able

to conceive during the betrothal period, the marriage would probably be a fruitful one. But because any child born prior to the actual wedding would legally be a bastard and denied rights of inheritance, it was important that the marriage take place before the child was born. If, however, the bride-to-be did not become pregnant, the marriage could always be called off; once again, good for the groom. As coldly businesslike as this all may seem, it does illustrate two important points: Living together is hardly a modern phenomenon, and medieval marriages were primarily ceremonial.

Assuming that the prenuptial period went well and everyone was happy with the arrangements, the date for the wedding would be set, and preparations for the big day would begin in earnest.

The wedding feast could take place at the home of either party's family. A portion of the expenses might be taken out of the bride's dowry, but the rules seem to have been flexible. What we do know is that throughout the Middle Ages, there were no decorations or clothes specific to weddings. Weddings were simply one more occasion for which everyone brought out the best silver and put on his or her best clothes. In the case of the nobility and the very rich merchant class, new clothes probably would have been ordered, but they were not any different in design than the best fashion of the day, except for the fact that a bride would never wear white. Considering the cost of good clothes, it was imperative that they be worn more than once.

If the couple was of high enough status, members of the groom's party often dressed in matching livery. For the 1234 wedding of France's nineteen-year-old King Louis IX and thirteen-year-old Marguerite Berenger, the king's party was all dressed in purple, scarlet, and green robes trimmed in ermine. Their belts were enameled in gold, and on their heads they wore "cloth of gold" caps trimmed with peacock feathers. No record seems to survive as to what Marguerite wore, but then, she was just the daughter of a count, not the king of France.

The more important the celebrants, the grander the procession to the church. For King Louis's and Marguerite's nuptials, the wedding party rode in procession from the king's hunting lodge at Fontainebleau to the cathedral in Paris. While the number and splendor of the wedding party may have been particularly grand, the order in which the guests rode would have been the same at a wedding of any notable people. The

For those lucky enough to have a castle nearby, a medieval wedding can make the age of chivalry come to life. PHOTO BY PETER SAMWORTH

parade was led by a troupe of minstrels playing flutes, viols, trumpets, drums, and bagpipes. Behind the musicians came the bridal couple, followed by their parents. Usually the groom's family rode before the bride's. In this case, Louis's mother, the dowager queen, rode ahead of the bride's parents. In instances where the bride's family was of much higher status than the groom's, this order would probably be reversed. If there was a best man, a tradition more popular in Italy and Spain than elsewhere in Europe, he would probably ride between the bride and groom and their families. The positioning of the best man in the wedding procession was dictated by the reason for his existence. He was the "best" man because he was the best swordsman the groom could find—often a hired position—and it was his job to see to it that no one decided to make a last-minute attempt to stop the wedding.

At last the grand parade reached the church, and everyone dismounted, the gentlemen helping the ladies off their horses. As they re-formed on the walkway leading to the church, the bride was escorted by her father or guardian, and the groom was joined by the best man, just to be sure nothing nasty happened. As the parties approached the church doors, the priest, bearing the wedding ring, came outside and waited under the portico for everyone to approach. The church doors were usually closed behind him.

When the bride, the groom, and their attendants stood in front of the priest, he began to question them. Were they old enough to legally marry? Did they swear that they were not related in such a way that it would prevent them marrying? Did their parents consent to the marriage? Had they published the bans of their marriage, and had an appropriate time elapsed since the publication of the bans to allow anyone who objected to step forward? Did they both freely enter into the marriage? The last two of these questions are largely ceremonial today, but during the Middle Ages, this was the last chance to stop what might be an illegal or forced marriage.

With the legalities out of the way, the church provost, a lawyer, or the groom himself would read aloud the list of dowry arrangements: what the bride was bringing, what the groom was offering, and the terms and arrangements for payment. With the dowry having been read, the groom presented the bride with a small bag of coins, usually thirteen in number, which she would distribute to the poor. This was not a symbolic act of buying the woman, but showed that she was empowered to act in financial matters on her new husband's behalf.

The bride's father then relinquished hold of his daughter, and the groom took her right hand in his as they began to repeat their vows or, as it was known, "plight their troth." The troth plighted by Sir William Plumpton in 1450 was strikingly similar to modern wedding vows: "Here I take thee, Jhennet, to be my wedded wife, to hold and to have, at bed and at board, for fairer or lather (uglier), for better or worse, in sickness and in health, to death us depart, and thereto I plight my troth."

Attendants hold a canopy above the bridal couple during the mass.

After the groom had completed his vow—the bride remained silent throughout the ceremony—the priest delivered a short sermon on the sanctity of marriage and how it is the natural state in which man and woman should live their lives. References were often made to idyllic biblical marriages and to the fact that the pairs of animals that went into Noah's ark were actually married in the sight of God, and that is why they, rather than other animals, were spared from the flood. The priest would then bless the ring, which he had been holding, and hand it to the groom, who slipped it, one by one, on the first three fingers of the bride's left hand. As the ring moved from finger to finger, the groom said: "In the name of the Father, and of the Son, and of the Holy Ghost, with this ring, I thee wed." The use of the third finger on the left hand is explained in a sermon that has survived from the fourteenth century. Bear in mind that the thumb is here considered a finger, so it is the fourth finger, rather than the third, that is mentioned. The sermon says that the ring must be "put and set by the husband upon the fourth finger of the woman, to show that a true love and cordial affection be between them, because, as doctors say, there is a vein coming from the heart of a woman to the fourth finger, and therefore the ring is put on the same finger, so that she should keep unity and love with him, and he with her." A bride did not present a ring to her husband until the sixteenth century. With the completion of the ring ceremony, the civil portion of the ceremony was concluded.

The vows having been said, the bride distributed the coins to the poor or gave them to the priest to distribute as he saw fit, the church doors were thrown open, and the wedding party entered the church for mass. The fact that the vows took place outside the church showed that although the wedding was sanctified and legitimized by the clergy, it was still primarily a civil rite. It was the acceptance and acknowledgment of the public that was of utmost importance.

Inside the church, everyone took his or her place in the pews while the bride, groom, two attendants, and the best man (if there was one) followed the priest to the altar. As the couple knelt in front of the priest, the attendants opened a large cloth over their heads to form a canopy, which would remain in place throughout the mass. The best man stood to the side of the groom. When the mass was finished, the canopy was removed from above the couple, and the priest gave the groom the "kiss of peace," which the groom then transferred to his new wife. The priest closed the service with a blessing for the new couple. One such blessing that survives goes as follows: "Let this woman be amiable as Rachel, wise as Rebecca, faithful as Sarah. Let her be sober through truth, venerable through modesty and wise through the teachings of heaven." As the couple processed out of the church, the choir traditionally chanted the "Angus Dei," a copy of which is included in chapter 13.

The members of the wedding party remounted their horses and followed the musicians as they wended their way to the wedding feast. The feast hall was laid out in the same fashion as described in chapter 2. Among the rushes that were usually scattered on the floor of the hall were strewn flowers, especially roses and lilies. Not only did the flowers add a festive flair to the room, but each time they were trod on, their scent was released into the air. The flowers and the long tables set with the finest silver and pewter the family owned were all fine and grand, but as at all medieval banquets, the center of attention was the food. At the 1376 wedding feast of wealthy, forty-year-old Italian merchant Francesco di Marco Datini and his sixteen-year-old bride Margherits Bandini, the shopping list included 406 loaves of bread, 250 eggs, 100 pounds of cheese, two quarters of oxen and sixteen of mutton, thirty-seven capons, eleven chickens, two boar's heads, innumerable pigeons and waterfowl, as well as wines imported from Provence, France, and Chianti from Tuscany. Based on the quantity of food here and the probability that the wedding feast lasted the traditional three days, we can assume that the wedding party must have numbered between fifty and sixty people.

At the feast, the bride and groom were normally allowed the honor of the central seats at high table, even though, in most cases, their parents would have outranked them. The feast was formally opened by the bride and groom drinking from a goblet especially commissioned for the occasion. The groom drank first, then passed the cup to his bride to finish. They were to be the only two people who ever drank from this cup, which was to be used only this once. Traditionally, this cup had two handles on it—not unlike a modern trophy—and came to be known as a "loving cup" or a "love cup."

Between food courses, the entertainments were interspersed with rounds of gift giving. Guests would present the newlyweds with gifts in much the same manner as they do today, although it was traditional for female members of the groom's family to present the new bride with rings. Not only was jewelry an appropriate gift in a time before electric blenders and pop-up toasters, but the ring symbolized the bride's being welcomed into the family of the groom. In many instances, the same rings were passed on to new brides generation after generation as a symbol of the continuity of family unity through successive generations. The guests often expected to receive gifts in return. Although seldom more than tokens of appreciation, these gifts had to reflect the social status of the recipient, not the giver.

During Italian wedding receptions, it was customary to place a gold florin (a coin) in the shoe of the new bride and a baby in her arms. Both of these tokens were in the hopes of future fertility. At the end of the first day's feasting, when everyone had wished the new couple many years of happiness filled with innumerable children, their future connubial bliss was given a proper inauguration by the entire company. Once the marital bed was made ready by the servants and sprinkled with rose petals, the company escorted the couple to their bedchamber. In separate anterooms, the bride and groom were undressed by their closest friends or servants and dressed in their best nightclothes. When they were ready, they were ushered into their bedchamber and put into bed in front of as many family members and friends as could squeeze into the bedroom. The priest then blessed the bed and the happy couple in a ceremony that would hopefully ensure fertility and remove any taint of premarital promiscuity from the bride (male peccadillos didn't seem to count). In most instances, the priest then said a benediction, and the company withdrew to leave the couple to consummate their marriage in private, but there were exceptions to every rule. Occasionally, even among the nobility, wedding-night sex became a public spectacle.

During the Middle Ages, as at any period, wedding customs varied according to regional, local, and family traditions. The above should, however, provide you with a good overview of the complicated process through which a betrothed couple had to make their way to complete their wedding ceremony. Some of the movies listed in the filmography contain weddings; they are marked with an asterisk (*) for easy reference. Do not assume that they are accurate representations of a medieval wedding, but they may offer some ideas.

THE TWELFTH-CENTURY MASS

The mass below includes staging directions, very much as it would have been performed during the Middle Ages. This is the Sarum mass used in England, not the post-Reformation Roman Catholic mass. Although it is no longer practiced, it is still an official form of the mass and should be acceptable as a part of any church ceremony, including a wedding. Consult your local priest as to specific proprieties.

Note: The performance of the mass requires two persons. Here they are listed as the priest (P) and a monk (M), as they would have been in the Middle Ages. Your priest will know the appropriate substitution for the part of the monk.

Remember that church Latin is completely phonetic. For example, Tuum is pronounced "too-um."

Priest and monk process toward altar.

P ASPERGES ME DOMINE, HYSSOPO ET MUNDABOR LAVABIS ME, ET SUPER NIVEM DEALBABOR.

Purge me, Oh Lord, with hyssop and I shall be clean. Thou shall wash me and I shall be whiter than snow.

M MISERERE MEI DEUS, SECUNDUM MAGNAM MISERICORDIAM TUAM.

Have mercy on me, Oh God, after Thy great goodness.

P GLORIA PATRI ET FILIO ET SPIRITUI SANCTO.

Glory to the Father, the Son, and the Holy Spirit.

M ASPERGES ME DOMINE, HYSSOPO ET MUNDABOR LAVABIS ME, ET SUPER NIVEM DEALBABOR.

Purge me, Oh Lord, with hyssop* and I shall be clean. Thou shall wash me and I shall be whiter than snow.

P OSTENDE NOBIS DOMINE MISERICORDIAM TUAM.

Show Thy mercy unto us, Oh Lord.

M ET SALUTARE TUUM DA NOBIS.

And grant us Thy salvation.

P DOMINE EXAUDI ORATIONEM MEAM.

Give thanks unto the Lord.

M ET CLAMOR MEUS AD TE VENIATE.

And let my cry come unto Thee.

P VIDI AQUAM EGREDIENTEM DE TEMPLO ALATARE DEXTRO.
ALLELUIA
ET OMNE AD QUOS PER VENIT AQUA
ISTA SALVI FACTI SUNT ET DICENT
ALLELUIA, ALLELUIA.

I saw water issuing out of the temple at the right hand side
Halleluia
and to all to whom that water came were made whole and shall say
Halleluia, Halleluia.

---

*Hyssop was an herb believed by medieval physicians to have great cleansing properties.

Priest then goes to altar, picks up bowl of holy water, takes sprinkler and sprinkles bride, groom, and congregation, then turns to altar, bows, and sprinkles altar. When he has finished, he puts holy water and sprinkler on the altar, bows, and crosses himself.

M	VENI CREATOR SPIRITUS	Come, Holy Spirit, inspire our souls
	MENTES TUORAM VISITA	and light them with celestial fire.
	IMPLE SUPERNA GRATIA	Thou art the anointing spirit
	QUAE TU CREASTI PECTORA	who imparts thy sevenfold gift.
	QUI PARACLETUS DICERIS	Thy blessed gift from above
	DONUM DEI ALTISSIMI	is the comfort of life and the fire of love
	FONS VIVUS IGNIS CARITAS	to enlighten with perpetual light
	ET SPIRITALIS UNCTIO	the dullness of our blinded sight.

While the monk has been chanting, the priest has been putting on the chasuble, a sleeveless outer vestment.

P	EMITTE SPIRITUM TUUM	Come, Holy Spirit
M	ET RENOUABIS FACIEUM TERRE	and renew the face of the earth.
P	DEUS CUI OMNE COR PATET	Oh Lord, to whom all hearts are open,
	ET OMNIS VOLUNTAS LOQUITUR	all desires known,
	ET QUEM NULLUM LATET SECRETUM	and from whom no secrets are hid,
	PURIFICA PER INFUSIONEM SANCTI SPIRITUS	cleanse the thoughts of our hearts
	COGITATIONES CORDIS ET DIGNE	by the inspiration of thy Holy Spirit.
	LAUDARE MEREAMUR	
P	PSALMUS QUADRAGINTA DUO JUDICA ME DEUS	Pass judgment on my side, Oh God.
M	(Reads Psalm 42 in English)	(Reads Psalm 42 in English.)
P	GLORIA PATRI ET FILLIO ET SPIRITUI SANCTO	Glory to the Father, the Son, and the Holy Spirit.
M	SICUT ERAT IN PRINCIPIO ET NUNC	As it was in the beginning, is now,
	ET SEMPER ET IN SECULA SECULORUM	and shall be ever more,
	AMEN	Amen
P	KYRIE ELEISON, CHRISTI ELEISON, KYRIE ELEISON	Lord have mercy, Christ have mercy, Lord have mercy.
M	KYRIE ELEISON, CHRISTI ELEISON, KYRIE ELEISON	Lord have mercy, Christ have mercy, Lord have mercy.
P	KYRIE ELEISON, CHRISTI ELEISON, KYRIE ELEISON	Lord have mercy, Christ have mercy, Lord have mercy.
	OREMUS	Let us pray.

P	PATER NOSTER	Our Father
	QUI ES IN CAELIS	who art in heaven
	SANCTIFICETUR NOMEN TUUM	Hallowed be thy name
	ADVENIAT REGNUM TUUM	Thy Kingdom come
	FIAT VOLUNTAS TUA	Thy will be done
	SICUT IN CAELO ET IN TERRA	in earth as it is in heaven
	PANEM NOSTRUM COTIDIANUM DA NOBIS HODIE	Give us this day our daily bread
	ET DIMITTE NOBIS DEBITA NOSTRA	And forgive us our trespasses
	SICUT ET NOS DIMITTIMUS DEBITORIBUS NOSTRIS	As we forgive those who trespass against us
	ET NE NOS INDUCAS IN TENTATIONEM	And lead us not into temptation
	SED LIBERA NOS A MALO	But deliver us from evil
	AMEN	Amen
M	AUFER A NOBIS DOMINE DEUS	Take from us, Oh Lord God,
	CINCTAS INIQUITATES NOSTRAS	the sins which encompass us;
	UT AD SANCTA SANCTORUM PARIS MENTIBUS	that with untroubled minds
	MEREAMUR INTROIRE	we may be worthy to enter the Holy of Holies;
	PER CHRISTUM DOMINUM NOSTRUM	through Christ our Lord.
P	CONFITEOR DEO OMNIPOTENTI	I confess to God,
	BEATI MARIA SEMPER VIRGINI	the Blessed Holy Virgin Mary,
	BEATO MICHAELI ARCHANGELO	and the Blessed Archangel Michael
P	BEATO JOANNI BAPTISTAE	Blessed John the Baptist,
	SANCTI APOSTOLIS PETRO ET PAULO	Holy Apostles Peter and Paul,
	OMNIBUS SANCTIS ET TIBI PATER	to all the saints and to You, Father,
	QUIA PECCAVI NIMIS COGITATIONE	that I have sinned in thought,
	VERBO ET OPERE	word, and deed.

Priest strikes breast three times, saying,

P	MEA CULPA, MEA CULPA, MEA MAXIMA CULPA	I have sinned, I have sinned, I have most grievously sinned.
P	IDEO PRECOR BEATAM MARIAM SEMPER VIRGINI	Therefore, I pray the Blessed Mary, ever Virgin,
	ET TE PATER ORARE PRO ME AD DOMINUM	and You, Father, to pray for me to the Lord
	DEUM NOSTRUM	our God.

Priest turns to face congregation and then crosses himself.

P	MISEREATUR VESTRI OMNIPOTENS DEUS	May Almighty God have mercy on you
	ET DIMISSIS PECCATIS VESTRIS	and deliver you from your sins,
	PERDUCAT VOS AD VITAM AETERNAM	and bring you everlasting life.
	AMEN	Amen

Priest makes sign of cross in the air, turns to the altar, then turns to a second monk carrying an incense burner, who has moved forward. Priest bows to the incense bearer, who bows back. Priest then moves to one side, and incense bearer incenses the altar to the right, left, middle, and back to the right again.

Priest goes to altar and kisses altar top.

P AB ILLO BENEDICARIS IN CUJUS HONORE
    CREMABERIS AMEN

May you be blessed by Him in whose honour
you shall be burned. Amen

The Gloria, below, can be sung.

M GLORIA IN EXCELSIS DEO
    ET IN TERRA PAX
    HOMINIBUS BONAE VOLUNTATIS
    LAUDAMUS TE
    BENEDICIMUS TE
    ADORAMUS TE

Glory be to God on high
and in earth, peace,
goodwill toward men.
We praise Thee,
We bless Thee,
We worship Thee.

M GLORIFACAMUS TE
    GRATIA AGIMUS TIBI
    PROPTER MAGNAM GLORIAM TUAM
    DOMINE DEUS REX CAELESTIS DEUS
    PATER OMNIPOTENS
    DOMINE FILI, UNIGENITE JESU CHRISTE
    DOMINE DEUS AGNUS DEI
    FILIUS PATRI
    QUI TOLLIS PECCATA MUNDI
    MISERERE NOBIS

We glorify Thee
We give thanks to Thee
for Thy great Glory
Oh King of heaven, Lord God,
Father Almighty
God the Son, the only begotten Jesus Christ,
the Lamb of God,
Son of the Father,
who takest away the sins of the world,
receive our prayer and have mercy on us.

P QUI TOLLIS PECCATA MUNDI SUSCIPE
    DEPRECATIONEM NOSTRAM
    QUI SEDES AD DEXTRAM PATRIS
    MISERERE NOBIS
    QUONIAM TU SOLUS SANCTUS
    TU SOLUS ALTISSIMUS JESU CHRISTE
    CUM SANCTO SPIRITU IN GLORIA DEI PATRIS
    AMEN

Thou that takest away the sins of the world
receive our prayer
You who sit at the right hand of God the Father,
have mercy upon us.
For You alone are holy,
You alone Jesus Christ, are most high
with the Holy Spirit in the Glory of God the Father.
Amen

Monk now reads a Collect, a call to worship that changes with the particular holy day or saint's day, in English.

P DOMINUS SIT IN CORDE TUO ET IN LABIIS TUIS
    UT DIGNE ET COMPETENTER ANNUNTIES
    EVANGELIUM SUUM

May the Lord be in your heart and upon your lips
that you may worthily proclaim
His evangelic greatness.

Reader bows to altar, puts on a long vestment called a cope, takes Bible, and walks to other side of room, escorted by the incense bearer. At far end of room, the incense bearer incenses Bible and reader. Reader makes sign of cross in air over Bible.

M   SEQUENTA SANCTI EVANGELII SECUNDUM   The gospel according to (insert Gospel name here).

Monk now reads a selection in English from one of the Gospels, then says,

M   GLORIA TIBI DOMINE   Glory be to Thee, Oh Lord.

Monk crosses self, walks back to altar, bows, places Bible on the altar, removes cope, and returns to his place. Everyone turns to face altar.

P   CREDO   I believe
    CREDO IN UNUM DEUM PATREM OMNIPOTENTEM   I believe in one God, Father almighty,
    FACTOREM COELI ET TERRA VISIBLIUM   maker of heaven and earth
    OMNIUM, ET INVISIBILIUM   and all that is invisible
    ET IN UNUM DOMINUM JESU CHRISTI   and in one Lord, Jesus Christ,
    FILIUM DEI UNIGENTUM   the only begotten Son of God,
    ET EX PATRE NATUM ANTE OMNIA SECULA   and begotten of his Father before all worlds.
    DEUM DE DEO   God of God,
    LUMEN DE LUMINE   light of light,
    DEUM VERUM DEO VERO   very God of very God,
    GENITUM NON FACTUM CONSUBSTANTIALEM   begotten, not made, of one substance
    PATRI PER QUEM OMNIA FACTA SUNT   with the Father by whom all things were made,
    QUI PROPTER NOS HOMINES ET PROPTER   who for us and our salvation
    NOSTRAM SALUTEM DESCENDIT DE COELIS   came down from heaven.

Entire congregation kneels. Priest should allow thirty seconds before continuing.

P   ET INCARNATUS EST DE SPRIITU SANCTO   and was made incarnate by the Holy Spirit
    EX MARIA VIRGINEE ET HOMO FACTUS EST   of the Virgin Mary and was made man.
    CRUCIFIXUS ETIAM PRO NOBIS SUB PONTIO   He was crucified under Pontius Pilate,
    PILATO PASSUS ET SEPULTUS EST   suffered, and was buried,
    ET RESUR EXIT TERTIA DIE   and rose again on the third day
    SECUNDUM SCRIPTURAS   according to the Scriptures.

P	ET ASCENDIT IN COELUM		He ascended into heaven

P ET ASCENDIT IN COELUM — He ascended into heaven
SEDET AD DEXTERAM PATRIS — and sitteth at the right hand of the Father
ET ITERUM VENTURUS EST CUM GLORIA — and He shall come again with Glory
JUDICARE VIVOS ET MORTUOS: — to judge the quick and the dead.
CUIUS REGNI NON ERIT FINIS — His Kingdom shall have no end.
ET IN SPIRITUM SANCTUM — And in the Holy Spirit,
DOMINUM ET VIVIFICANTEM — the Lord and giver of life
QUI EX PATRE FILIOQUE PROCEDIT — who proceedeth from the Father and the Son,
QUI CUM PATRE ET FILIO SIMUL ADORATUR — who with the Father and Son is worshipped
ET CONGLORIFACTUR — and glorified,
QUI LOCUTUS EST PER PROPHETAS — and spoken through the prophets,
ET UNAM SANCTAM CATHOLICAM ET — and in one Holy Catholic and
APOSTOLICUM ECCLESIAM — Apostolic Church.
CONFITEOR UNUM BAPTISMA IN REMISSIONEM — I acknowledge one baptism for the remission
PECCATORUM — of sins,
ET EXPECTO RESURRECTIONEM MORTUORUM — and I look for the resurrection of the dead
ET VITAM VENTURI SECULI — and of the life of the world to come.
AMEN — Amen

Everyone stands up.

P SUSCIPE SANCTA TRINITAS HANC OBLATIONEM — Receive, Oh Holy Trinity, this oblation
QUAM EGO MISER ET INDIGNUS OFFERO — which I, an unworthy sinner, offer
IN HONORE TUO ET BEATE MARIA PERPETUE — in Thy honour and in that of the Blessed Mary,
VIRGINIS — ever a virgin,
ET OMNIUM SANCTORUM TUORUM — and all the saints,
PRO PECCATIS MIES ET PRO SALUTE VIVORUM — for my sins and for the salvation of the living
ET REQUIE OMNIUM ET PRO SALUTE VIVORUM ET — and the repose of all the faithfully departed;
REQUIE OMNIUM FIDELIUM DEFUNTOREUM
QUI VIVIS ET REGNAS — Who lives and reigns for ever and ever

M IN SPIRITUS HUMILITATIS — In the spirit of humility
ET ANIMO I CONTRITO SUSCIPIAMUR — and with a contrite heart, may we be accepted,
DOMINE A TE — Oh Lord, by Thee
ET SIC FIAT SACRIFICIUM NOSTRUM UT A TE — and cause our sacrifice to be accepted as worthy
SUSCIPIATUR HODIE UT PLACEAT TIBI — in Thy sight that it may please Thee,
DOMINE DEUS — Oh Lord God.

From this point, a plus sign (+) means that the speaker crosses himself.

A bowl of water and a towel are now brought forward. The priest washes his hands and dries them on towel. The bowl is then removed.

P   DOMINUS VOBISCUM   The Lord be with thee,

M   ET CUM SPIRITU TUO   and with thy spirit.

P   SURSUM CORDA   Lift up your hearts,

M   HABEMUS AD DOMINUM   We lift them to our Lord God

P   GRATIAS AGIMUS DOMINO DEO NOSTRO   Let us give thanks to our Lord God.

M   DIGNUM ET JUSTUM EST   It is meet and right so to do.

The Sanctus, below, is sung.

P   SANCTUS SANCTUS SANCTUS   Holy, holy, holy
     DOMINE DEUS SABAOTH   Lord God of Hosts
     PLENI SUNT COELI ET TERRA GLORIA TUA   Heaven and earth are filled with Thy Glory

M   HOSANNA IN EXCELSIS   Hosanna in the highest

P   BENEDICTUS QUI VENIT IN NOMINE DOMINI   Blessed is he that cometh in the name of the Lord

M   HOSANNA IN EXCELSIS   Hosanna in the highest

P   TE IGITUR CLEMENTISSIME PATER   Therefore, most merciful Father
     PER JESUM CHRISTUM FILIUM TUUM   through Jesus Christ thy Son,
     DOMINUM NOSTRUM   our Lord
     SUPPLICES ROGAMUS AC PETIMUS UTI ACCEPTA   we humbly pray Thee to accept
     HABEAS ET BENEDICAS HAEC DONA (+)   and bless these gifts (+)
     HAEC MUNERA (+) HAEC SANCTA (+) SACRIFICIA   these presents (+) these holy (+) unblemished sacrifices
     ILLIBATA IN PRIMIS QUAE TIBI OFFERIMUS   which we offer to Thee
     PRO ECCLESIA TUA SANCTA CATHOLICA   on behalf of Thy holy Catholic Church
     QUAM PACIFICARE CUSTODIRE ADUNARE   which you promise to keep in peace
     ET REGERE DIGNERIS TOTO ORBE   and govern throughout the whole world
     TERRARUM UNA CUM FAMULO TUO PAPA NOSTRO   together with Thy servant, our Pope
     (insert Pope's name)   (insert name),
     ET ANTISTE NOSTRO (insert local Bishop's name)   our Bishop (insert name),
     ET REGE (insert name of monarch or president)   and our King (name of monarch or president),
     ET OMNIBUS   and all

P ORTHODOXIS ATQUE CATHOLICE ET APOSTOLICE
    FIDEI CULTORIBUS
    MEMENTO DOMINE FAMULORUM
    FAMULARUMQUE TUARUM
    (here insert names of bride and groom)
    ET OMNIUM CIRCUMSTANTIUM QUORUM TIBI
    FIDES COGNITA EST NOTA DEVOTIO
    PRO QUIBUS TIBI OFFERIMUS. VEL QUI TIBI
    OFFERUNT HOC SACRIFICIUM LAUDIS PRO SE
    SUISQUE OMNIBUS
    PRO REDEMPTIONE ANIMARUM SUARUM
    PRO SPE SALUTIS ET INCOLUMITATIS SUAE
    TIBI REDDUNT UOTA SUA
    ETERNO DEO VIVO ET VERO

who are Orthodox, and who hold the Catholic
and Apostolic faith
remember, Oh Lord, Thy servant
and Thy handmaiden
(insert names)
and all here present whose faith is approved
and whose devotion is known to Thee
on behalf of whom we offer unto Thee
this sacrifice of praise for themselves
and all theirs,
and the redemption of their souls
for the hope of their salvation and their security,
who make these vows unto You
the eternal, living God.

M COMMUNICATNES ET VENERENTES
    IN PRIMIS GLORIOSAE SEMPER VIRGINIS MARIA
    GENITRICIS DIE ET DOMINE NOSTRI JESU CHRISTI
    SED ET BEATORUM APOSTOLORUM AC
    MARTYRUM TUORUM PETRI, PAULO ANDREAE
    (here add the names of any saints who are special to the
    couple or the saint whose feast day is nearest)
    ET OMNIUM SANCTORUM TUORUM QUORUM
    MERITIS PRECIBUSQUE CONCEDAS UT IN OMNIBUS
    PROTECTIONIS TUAE MUNIAMUR AUXILIO
    PER EUENDEM CHRISTUM DOMINUM NOSTRUM
    AMEN

In communicating and reverencing
with the glorious and ever virgin Mary,
Mother of our God and Lord Jesus Christ
and also of Thy blessed apostles
and martyrs Peter, Paul, Andrew
(add saint names)

And all Thy Saints through whose prayers
and merits Thou grant that in all things
we may be defended by the aid of Thy protection.
Through the same Christ our Lord
Amen

P HANC IGITUR OBLATIONEM SERVITUTIS NOSTRAE
    SED ET CUNCT FAMILIAE TUAE QUAESUMIS
    DOMINE UT PLACATUS ACCIPIAS DIESQUE
    NOSTROS IN TUA PACE DISPONAS
    ATQUE AB ETERNA DAMNATIONE NOS
    ERIPI ER IN ELECTORUM TUORUM JUBEAS

Therefore, Oh Lord, graciously accept this oblation
of our service and of Thy whole family,
we beseech Thee, Oh Lord,
dispose our days in Thy peace,
and that we may be delivered from eternal damnation
and be numbered among the flock of Thine elect.

P GREGE NUMERARI PER CHRISTUM DOMINUM
    NOSTRUM
    AMEN

Through Christ our Lord

Amen

P QUAM OBLIATION TU DUES IN OMNIBUS
    QUAESUMUS
    BENEDICTAM (+) ADSCRIPTAM (+)
    RATAM RATIONABILEM ACCEPTABILEMQUE
    FACERE DIGNERIS UT NOBIS CORPUS (+)
    ET SANGUIS (+) FIAT DILECTISSIMI FILII
    DOMINI NOSTRI JESU CHRISTI

Which oblation, we beseech Thee,
Oh God
to bless (+) approve (+)
ratify and make reasonable and acceptable,
that it may become to us the body (+)
and blood (+) of Thy most dearly beloved Son,
our Lord, Jesus Christ

Priest bows to altar, bends knee, and kisses altar top.

P   QUI PRIDIE QUAM PATERETUR ACCEPIT,
       PANEM IN SANCTAS ET VENERABLIES MANUS SUAS
       BENEDIXIT AC FREGIT DEDITQUE DISCIPULIS SUIS
       DICENS

Who, the day before he suffered,
took bread into His holy hands,
blessed it, broke it and gave it to His disciples
saying:

Priest picks up Host on paten and raises above his head. Monk rings bell three times. Priest places Host on altar and puts hands over Host.

P   ACCIPITE ET MANDUCATE EX HOC OMNES HOC
       EST ENIM CORPUS MEUM

Take and eat ye all, of this,
for this is My body

Monk rings bell three times.
Priest bows to altar, then pours wine into chalice, which is sitting on right side of altar.

P   SIMILI MODO POSTEA QUAM CENATUM EST
       ACCIPIENS ET HUNC PRAECLARUM CALICEM
       IN SANCTAS AC VENERABILIS MANUS SUAS
       ITEM TIBI GRACIAS AGENS BENEDIXIT (+)
       DEDITQUE SUIS DICENS

Likewise, after supper,
taking the chalice
in His holy and venerable hands
and giving thanks to Thee He blessed it (+)
and gave it to His disciples saying:

P   ACCEPITE ET BIBITE EX EO OMNES

Take and drink ye all, of this.

Priest raises chalice above head, replaces chalice on altar, and places hands over chalice.

P   HIC EST ENIM CALIX SANGUINIS MEI NOVI
       ET ETERNI TESTAMENTI
       MYSTERIUM FIDEI QUI PRO VOBIS ET PRO MUTIS
       EFFUNDETUR IN REMISSIONEM PECCATORUM
       HAEC QUOTIES CUMQUE FECERITIS
       IN MEI MEMORIAM FACIETIS

For this is the cup of My blood of the new
and everlasting testament,
the mystery of faith which shall be shed for you
and for many for the remission of sin.
As oft as ye do these things,
do them in remembrance of Me.

Monk rings bell three times.

P   PER IPSUM (+) ET CUM IPSO (+) ET IN IPSO (+)
       EST TIBI DEO PATRI (+) OMNIPOTENTI
       IN UNITATE SPIRITUS (+) SANCTI OMNIS HONOR
       ET GLORIA PER OMNIA SECULA SECULORUM
       AMEN

Through Him (+) and with Him (+) and in Him (+)
all honour and glory (+) is to Thee,
God the Father almighty (+) in the unity of the Holy
Spirit, for ever and ever.
Amen

M	PRECEPTIS SALUTARIBUS MONITI	Taught by saving precepts,
	DIVINA INSTITUTONE FORMATI	and divine institution,
	AUDEMUS DICERE	we dare to say:
	PATER NOSTER	Our Father
	QUI ES IN CAELIS	who art in heaven
	SANCTIFICETUR NOMEN TUUM	Hallowed be Thy name
	ADVENIAT REGNUM TUUM	Thy Kingdom come
	FIAT VOLUNTAS TUA	Thy will be done
	SICUT IN CAELO ET IN TERRA	in earth as it is in heaven
	PANEM NOSTRUM QUOTIDIANUM DA NOBIS HODIE	Give us this day our daily bread
	ET DIMITTE NOBIS DEBITA NOSTRA	And forgive us our trespasses
	SICUT ET NOS DIMITTIMUS DEBITORIBUS NOSTRIS	As we forgive those who trespass against us
	ET NE NOS INDUCAS IN TENTANTIONEM	And lead us not into temptation
	SED LIBERA NOS A MALO	But deliver us from evil.
	AMEN	Amen

Priest takes Host in hands, breaks it in half, puts one part on paten, then takes the other half and again breaks it in half.

P	HAEC COMMIXITIO ET CONSECRATIO CORPORIS	Let this most holy mixture and consecration of the body
	ET SANGUINIS DOMINI NOSTRI JESU CHRISTI	and blood of our Lord, Jesus Christ,
	FIAT ACCIPIENTIBUS NOBIS IN VITAM AETERNAM	be for us to receive it for everlasting life.
	AMEN	Amen

Priest takes one quarter of the Host, puts it in chalice with wine, eats other quarter, then strikes breast three times.

M	AGNUS DEI QUI TOLLIS PECCATA MUNDI	Lamb of God that taketh away the sins of the world,
	MISERERE NOBIS	have mercy on us.
	AGNUS DIE QUI TOLLIS PECCATA MUNDI	Lamb of God that taketh away the sins of the world,
	MISERERE NOBIS	have mercy on us
	AGNUS DEI QUI TOLLIS PECCATA MUNDI	
	DONA NOBIS PACEM	and grant us Thy peace.

Priest gives Host to bride and groom, saying,

P	CORPUS CHRISTI	Body of Christ
P	DOMINUS VOBISCUM	Lord be with you
M	ET CUM SPIRITU TUO	and with thy spirit
P	ITE MISSA EST	Go, the mass is ended

Priest turns to the congregation to give blessing.

P   BENEDICAT VOS OMNIPOTONS DEUS PATER   May almighty God, Father,
    ET FILIUS ET SPIRITUS SANCTUS   Son, and Holy Spirit, bless you.
    AMEN   Amen

Priest makes sign of cross in the air.

Wedded couple depart, followed by priest and monks. Everyone genuflects before leaving.

CHAPTER 6

DECORATING IN THE MEDIEVAL STYLE

To host a proper medieval feast, you must either have a proper medieval feast hall in which to hold it or create the feel and mood of a feast hall in your home or a rented space. Drawing on books and movies (see pages 141–144), create in your mind's eye the feast hall of a medieval castle. Start by visualizing the empty space—a huge, cavernous room with walls reaching up toward massive rafters of dark, ancient oak. As you walk across the heavy plank floor, the echo of your footsteps rolls softly around your ears. Now, begin to fill in the furnishings.

At the far end of the room is a massive table. At its center are two high-backed armchairs, flanked by several smaller chairs on either side. Along one wall is a heavily carved sideboard piled high with pewter and silver platters, bowls, and mugs. The other walls are covered with rich tapestries, banners displaying coats of arms, and arrangements of primitive, vicious-looking weapons. A soft light filters through windows set high in the walls, but the primary light comes from clusters of large candles set in tall, wrought-iron candelabra that stand in each corner of the room. In the distance, you can hear the nasal piping of medieval music.

Unfortunately, this room is imaginary. For your feast, you will have to transform whatever space you have available into a reasonable facsimile of a medieval banquet hall. If you are working with your own dining room, you are pretty well locked into the available floor space and ceiling height. A basement or garage might offer more room, however, and if you have access to a barn, it can be made to look far more medieval than any modern space. If you are considering a rented space, try to locate one that has the feel of a medieval

castle. This is not as hard as it might at first seem. Many towns have one or more Victorian Gothic churches with assembly halls that they are glad to rent out.

No matter what space you begin with, making it look and feel properly medieval will require some ingenuity. Tremendous amounts of medieval atmosphere can be added to even the most starkly modern space through judicious planning and a few days' work. If you are good with decorative crafts or can recruit someone who is handy to help you, all the better.

Start by planning the overall feel of the room in which the feast is to be held. Working with the colors that are already in the room, select properly medieval colors that will enhance the impact of the space. For a feel of medieval color schemes, look at the pictures of medieval rooms reproduced in the color section of this book. Medieval colors were rich and vibrant: ruby reds, emerald greens, rich blues, brilliant orange, and bright gold.

WALL DECORATION

No medieval feast hall is complete without great tapestries to adorn the walls. Armorial banners and painted wall hangings can be made to decorate your feast hall with as much or as little effort as you feel like putting into them.

The simplest wall hangings can be made from lengths of bold-colored upholstery fabric. Using the fabric in its full width, cut it to a length so that when hung on a wooden pole or drapery rod, it will extend from just below the ceiling to just above the floor. Several full widths of cloth in alternating colors, such as red and green, red and gold, or green and white, can be used to cover an entire wall. These alternating panels may be hung separately or sewn together to produce an unbroken wall hanging. To get a visual image of how this will look, turn to the photograph of Barley Hall in the color section of this book. Begin making the wall hangings by hemming all four edges of the tapestry. Then sew heavy gold upholstery fringe along the bottom edge. Along the top, sew a rod pocket, drapery rings, or lengths of cloth ribbon to tie the tapestry to the rod. Decorative finials on the rod will add to the visual effect. If you are using a space where you cannot or do not wish to attach drapery rods to the walls, fabric panels can be tacked directly to the wall with small nails or thumbtacks without inflicting noticeable damage on the walls.

More elaborate, painted wall hangings, with scenes of court life, hunting parties, or full-sized coats of arms, can be made with a few days to devote to the project. The more elaborate the design, the more time it will require. From lightweight canvas, a painter's dropcloth, or any fine-textured heavyweight cotton fabric (even bedsheets would work), cut banners of a size appropriate to the room in which they will hang, so that they will nearly cover the walls. Hem the edges to prevent fraying, and sew a rod pocket along the top if they are going to be hung on a rod. If these wall-size hangings seem too large to deal with, consider making a number of individual banners, each bearing a single coat of arms. These can be just as impressive as wall-size paintings and are far easier to make. You also have the advantage of being able to ask friends to paint one or two without overwhelming anyone.

When you have decided on the size and complexity of your wall decorations, locate a design for a coat of arms or a scene from a medieval manuscript illumination. A selection of coats of arms can be found in the color section of this book. Be sure the design is suitable to your level of artistic skills; for beginners, coats of arms are much safer than taking on a complex scene involving people, castles, and running horses. Sketch the design, full-size, on brown wrapping paper, newsprint, or butcher's paper until you are happy with it. Don't be afraid to fill the entire wall hanging with the design area. When the design is sketched out, you are ready to transfer it to the canvas. Position the drawing on the canvas, and pin it in place so it does not shift during the transfer process. Take a piece of paper and rub a very soft-leaded pencil across one side of it until the entire surface of the paper is covered. This will act as carbon paper to transfer the image from the paper to the canvas. Slide the "carbon paper," carbon side toward the canvas, between the drawing and the canvas. Trace over the drawing carefully with a ballpoint pen to transfer the image to the canvas. Do not use ordinary carbon paper; it is far too messy.

When the transfer is complete, paint in the image with latex-based interior wall paint or acrylic artist's paints. For complete instructions on reproducing more complex, medieval-style painted wall hangings, see *Constructing Medieval Furniture,* by Daniel Diehl (Stackpole Books, 1997).

If you are holding your feast in a space where there are exposed beams or open rafters, additional banners can be suspended from the ceiling for a strikingly medieval look. If possible, these banners should be confined to the long sides of the room and should be hung at a ninety-degree angle to the wall. Unlike

Painted wall hangings in the great hall of Barley Hall, York, England.

modern flags, which are often hung horizontally from ceiling beams, medieval banners were always hung vertically. This will also add to the visual height of the room. If your ceilings are less than ten feet in height, however, such banners may actually reduce the visual height of the room and should be avoided.

For those with more refined tastes and larger budgets, there are marvelous copies of medieval and Renaissance tapestries available from companies specializing in historical reproductions, such as Design Toscano, Schumacher Wallcoverings, or Braunschwig & Fils Wallcovering.

In those places where there are gaps between wall hangings or where walls are entirely exposed, remove any existing pictures and paintings, which were unknown during the Middle Ages and will make the room look less authentic.

WINDOW DECORATION
Most medieval windows were left bare. The only means of shutting out light and cold was by closing heavy wooden shutters. So leaving the windows in your recreated feast hall undecorated is entirely appropriate. If you want draperies, however, they should be made of a heavy fabric, either wool or velvet. If you want patterned draperies, select a heavy damask. Winter-weight bedspreads often have surprisingly medieval-looking damask patterns and can be adapted as window coverings with very little effort. Otherwise, panels of heavy, plain-colored upholstery fabric will work just as well. Choose your colors to correspond with one of the highlight colors in your wall hangings and banners. Once in place, swag the draperies to one side with heavy tiebacks or open them on an existing curtainrod. By all means, remove lace curtains and sheers, both of which are Victorian inventions.

Alternately, you might consider turning your windows into "stained-glass" works of art, keeping in mind that these are effective only if your dinner is to take place in the daytime. Stained-glass painting kits, complete with bright-colored glass paint and artificial lead, are available at many craft and hobby stores. Select an attractive coat of arms or scene from a medieval manuscript or from a stained-glass pattern book. If you do not want to paint directly on your windows because of the mess of removing the paint later, use a piece of Plexiglas that can be hung or screwed in place over the window frame and removed later. An easy and inexpensive way to get a stained-glass window effect is to use permanent markers on waxed paper.

Another idea for window treatment is to replicate the heavy wooden shutters that usually covered the windows of castles. Using sheets of plywood or perhaps even cardboard, cut panels to size and pierce them with an arbalestina, a cruciform arrow slot specifically designed for the use of crossbows. This cross-shaped cutout will allow light to enter the hall while masking any modern distractions outside the window.

FLOORS
Floors in medieval feast halls were either great slabs of stone or wooden planks. Though few homes today have flagstone floors, many have hardwood. If your home has natural wood floors, by all means roll up the area rugs and leave the floors bare. But if your dining room is carpeted, don't worry; the room will be so impressive when it is fully decorated that no one will notice.

The floors of feast halls in the Middle Ages were usually strewn with hay and sweet grasses to help keep the room warm and fresh smelling. Though this is not recommended for use on a carpeted floor, if you are holding your feast in a space with a tile, linoleum, or concrete floor, a light covering of hay will add significantly to the medieval atmosphere. If you choose to use hay on the floor, be sure to purchase hay, not straw, and only bring it in from outdoors a few hours before the feast to ensure that it does not dry out and become dusty. Sprinkling some potpourri around in the hay will add a pleasant scent to the room. Be careful to keep hay and any other combustible material well away from open flames and candles.

FEAST TABLES
The most important visual element in recreating the medieval feast is having proper-looking feast tables. Variations in the arrangement of tables in the feast hall were almost endless, but in all cases there was a designated high table, where the host and hostess, along with the highest-ranking visitors, were set apart from the rest of the guests. The hosts—or highest-ranking guests, if they were more noble than the hosts—were seated in the middle of the high table. Some high tables were placed on a raised platform, or dais, to elevate the heads of the nobility slightly above the rest of the company, giving the guests a good view of the nobility, their fine clothes, and refined manners. Because the medieval feast revolved around those seated at the high table, the rest of the guests had to be given an unobstructed view of their hosts. Chairs

were traditionally kept on one side of the high table so everyone there would be in full view of the rest of the room. The most honored among the company would be seated on massive, high-backed armchairs, those next in rank would have armchairs with lower backs, and toward the ends of the table were chairs with no arms.

Other tables in the hall were arranged in long rows, at a ninety-degree angle to the high table, so guests could look down the length of their tables toward the high table. Even at these lower tables, seating was all important; the closer a person was to the high table, the greater his or her rank and status. Those nearest the high table often had small, armless chairs, farther down the tables were individual stools, and at the ends of the tables were common benches.

The variety of seating used during the Middle Ages makes it all the easier to reproduce the feel of the medieval feast. Standard dining-room chairs can serve as the seating at the high table. If your chairs have high backs and are fairly simple in design, so much the better. If you have carver chairs with arms, these can be the seats of honor at the center of the table. Seating at the lower tables can be a mixture of folding chairs (wooden ones look better than metal) placed nearest the high table and picnic benches farther down the tables. Interestingly, the long benches used at medieval feast tables were called bankettes, and it is from this word that we derived the term *banquet*.

Most of the remaining tables in the great hall were portable affairs that could be taken apart and removed from the hall as the occasion demanded. For these "lower" tables, use rented folding tables. For serious do-it-yourselfers, old doors, heavy planks, or thirty-inch-wide sheets of three-quarter-inch plywood set on sawhorses all make good period substitutes.

If you have a large room for your feast, try to approximate the seating arrangement of the medieval feast hall by placing additional tables at right angles to the high table. Depending on the size of your feast, one row of additional seating can be placed directly in front of the high table, so the two tables form a T arrangement (see table diagram A). The top bar of the T should always serve as the high table. An alternative version of the T-shaped arrangement is the L. By moving the lower table off to one side of the high table, the majority of the floor space in the room is left open for dance and theatrical performances that might take place between removes. If you are having a really large

feast, arrange three lines of tables in a U shape (see table diagram B). The bottom of the U is the high table, and two additional rows of tables extend from either end. This arrangement is particularly nice because it allows the presentation of the food, as well as any entertainment, to take place in the center of the U, in full view of the entire company. If you use the U-shaped arrangement, you can have seating at one or both sides of the lower tables. If there is seating only along one side of the lower tables, everyone in the hall will be offered an unobstructed view of all the guests as well as the entertainment. If you have seating on both sides of these tables, as long as everyone can see those at the high table, you have a satisfactory medieval arrangement. Under no circumstances should there be seating on both sides of the high table.

If your room is too long and narrow to allow for a T- or U-shaped arrangement, seat your guests at one long table or two short tables placed end-to-end. Seat everyone along one side and both ends of the table, with the seats of honor being in the middle of the table. If necessary, people may sit on both sides of the table, but the area directly across from the "nobility" should be left open. The seats of these "nobles" can be distinguished by overlaying the main tablecloth with a secondary, contrasting cloth at the places of honor. The secondary cloth should hang over the front edge of the table at least as far as the primary cloth. For small, intimate medieval banquets where there is no separate high table, the seats of the hosts should stand apart from those of their guests by placing a secondary tablecloth in front of them.

No matter what the physical arrangement of the tables, the table coverings should be selected so that the high table always stands out from the others. One type of cloth may be plain and others patterned, or one white and others colored. Traditionally, a white cloth with a heavily decorated overcloth would be used on the high table. Play off the colors already in the room, and consider the materials and colors in your recreated wall hangings and tapestries.

OTHER FURNITURE

Medieval decorating was spare and functional. Other than the tables and chairs, most great halls had only one main piece of furniture, the cup board. Similar to Victorian sideboards or modern buffets, the cup board had a chest-type base with doors or drawers, above which was a shelf unit for the display of pewter and silver platters, plates, and goblets.

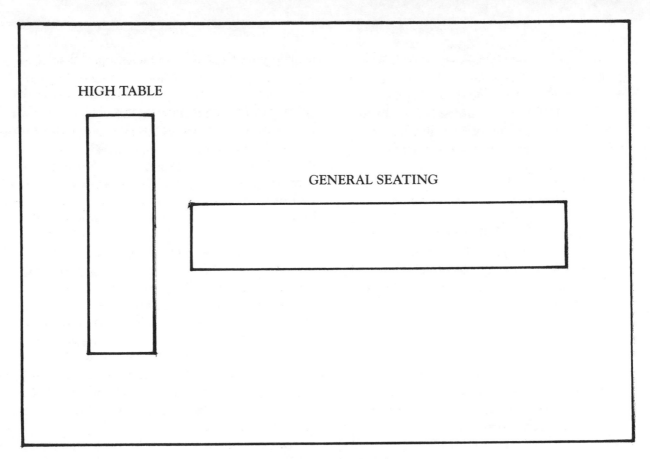

HIGH TABLE

GENERAL SEATING

TABLE DIAGRAM A

TABLE DIAGRAM B

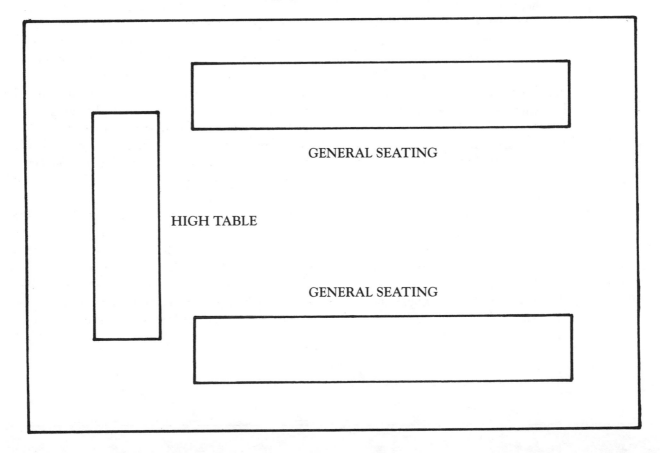

GENERAL SEATING

HIGH TABLE

GENERAL SEATING

If you have a traditional sideboard with shelves, so much the better. Remove china and glassware from the shelves and replace them with pewter and silver, or silver-colored, metal ware. Stainless serving platters, wooden bowls and plates, and pewter tankards or silver-plated stemware all make for a grand display.

Incidental furnishings like small side tables, knickknack shelves, and china cupboards should be removed, as such things did not exist during the Middle Ages.

A few trunks or wooden chests may be brought into the room to serve as appropriately medieval decoration and also to provide additional seating space. Chests and trunks were an ever-present part of medieval life and were used to store everything from clothing to written records to jewelry.

LIGHTING
Lighting in the medieval hall came from several sources. The crackling fire on the hearth, torches in iron wall brackets, and candles in great, floor-standing candelabra all played their part to brighten the vast, dark halls of castles and manor houses.

While we don't recommend that you have live torches hanging on the walls, a fire in the fireplace, if you are lucky enough to have one, is a great mood enhancer. The primary source of light for your recreated feast, however, should be candles. The most authentic-looking candles will be two or three inches in diameter and either white or natural beeswax color. Candles should be placed not only on the dining table, but also throughout the room to spread a soft, diffused light. If you have or can obtain floor-standing candlesticks, they are the ideal feast hall decoration.

Place drip catchers under any candles. The best drip catcher is a large, sand-filled tray that covers the entire area beneath the candelabra; this will guarantee that neither hot wax nor flame falls on carpeting, hardwood floors, or hay. Make sure not to place open flames close to draperies or decorations.

If possible, avoid the use of ceiling lights unless you have chandeliers that look like candles. In that case, use fifteen- or twenty-watt bulbs, which will provide adequate light without overpowering the candles. Another alternative to electric lights is to use one or two kerosene lamps. Although they are certainly not

medieval, the shimmering glow of a live flame is vastly preferable to electric lighting.

CHRISTMAS DECORATIONS
During the Middle Ages, Christmas decorations as we know them did not exist. There were, however, efforts made to make the great hall look decorative for the occasion and to help dispel the gloom of winter. So if your medieval feast is to take place over the Christmas holidays, there are a few extra things you should do to prepare.

When your feast hall has taken on a properly medieval look, it is time to add the festive trimmings appropriate to the holiday season. Not only did the addition of greenery bring a festive air to the great hall, but its scent freshened the musty air that was an inevitable result of large numbers of unwashed people living in cramped quarters. Mistletoe, with its supposed powers of love, brought the promise of new birth and spring, while the prickly holly leaves reminded the revelers of Christ's crown of thorns and the true reason for their celebrations.

Branches of evergreen or pre-made pine roping can be draped in large swags from ceiling cornices and beams and around door and window frames. Ceiling lights can also be draped with pine bows to disguise their presence. Additional greenery can be laid on dining tables and buffets as inexpensive centerpieces that add greatly to the primitive atmosphere of the medieval hall. Long-needled evergreens such as Austrian pine make the best decoration; not only do they provide the greatest amount of foliage for the money, but they have the most pungent scent and shed less than the short-needled variety. Mix sprigs of mistletoe, holly, ivy, and boxwood among the pine bows to provide visual texture. The bright red berries of holly are particularly effective punctuation to the greenery and should be used liberally. "Deck the hall" to your heart's content.

Surprisingly, the manger scene, with Joseph, Mary, the baby Jesus, shepherds, and wise men, was in common use during the Middle Ages, and the presence of a Nativity scene in a medieval setting is not at all out of place. Usually made of fired clay, the figures were normally left unpainted. Further information on Christmas decorating and traditions is given in chapter 4.

CHAPTER 7
MEDIEVAL MANNERS

◆

Popular myth often envisions medieval feasts as bacchanalias where bones were thrown on the floor to be eaten by the dogs and drunken brawls were an expected part of the evening's entertainment. Little could be farther from the truth. Medieval society demanded strict adherence to codes of chivalry in war and peace, to showing absolute respect toward women, and to proper observation of religious duties at all times—not a social structure likely to sanction drunken orgies at the dinner table. Medieval table manners, if not as complex and rigid as those of the Victorians, were certainly more structured than our own.

As much fun as most people have trying to eat medieval style, you may find youngsters reluctant to take part. We find that children often enjoy playing the part of peasants at medieval feasts so they don't have to dress as fancy or sit at the same tables as their parents, who are embarrassing them by acting abnormally, anyhow. Let the youngsters sit at a table, or on the floor, at the far end of the hall, and as peasants they are not expected to have all the manners of the gentry, giving them a little latitude to behave in ways not normally acceptable to medieval diners.

TABLE SETTING
To a great extent, table manners in any culture are established by the utensils with which food is served and consumed. In the broadest sense, the tableware available to medieval cooks, servers, and diners was not a great deal different from that used today, although the differences that did exist were fairly major. But first, let us look at the table as it appeared to the arriving guests.

At the center of the high table, in front of the highest-ranking person or couple, was the salt cellar, which served as a symbol of status and hospitality. Salt cellars usually took the form of a large, ornate cup, but some took the form of other objects like a small chest, an animal, or even a ship. In front of each seat in the hall was a soup bowl made of wood or pewter, and between each pair of seats was a small plate of similar material. Plates were pretty much reserved for fruits or the occasional vegetable, and one plate was normally shared by two people.

The medieval equivalents of dinner plates were called trenchers and were usually made of stale bread. Trencher loaves, either round or square, were allowed to go stale for four or five days before being used. If the trencher loaf was round, it would be cut horizontally into two round "dishes." The rounded surface of the top crust sometimes had to be cut away to allow the trencher to rest on the table without rocking. The top halves of the trencher loaves were always served to the most noble among the company, and from this practice came the term "upper crust" as a reference to the

A table setting as it might have appeared in the fourteenth or fifteenth century. Note the aquamanaile wine pitcher; bread trenchers set on wooden plates; individual soup bowls; a shared pewter plate for fruit, cheese, and vegetable; and a shared wine goblet. The spoon on the left is made of pewter, the one on the right is of horn. The knife on the left is a gentleman's belt knife, and on the right is a lady's table knife, sometimes also worn on the belt. All of these items are modern and can be found in specialty stores or through dealers in medieval reproduction goods.

wealthy elite. From these trenchers, solid foods like roasts, thick stews, and meat pies were eaten. If you use rectangular loaves, after allowing the bread to go stale, slice the loaf into one-inch-thick slices. Place five slices in front of each diner, with four slices arranged into a square and the fifth placed on top to keep the food and juices from dripping between the slices. Prepackaged pizza shells, large pita, or Indian nan breads can also be used as trenchers. In some instances, the bread trenchers were placed on wooden plates to protect the tablecloth from seeping juice. If you are concerned about staining your linen, feel free to do the same. Nine-inch metal pizza trays make perfectly acceptable trencher plates.

Medieval dinner guests were traditionally divided into pairs, who shared more than just a salad plate. Like plates, drinking vessels fell into the category of shared property. After drinking, a person wiped the rim of the cup with his or her napkin before replacing it on the table. Wine was consumed from heavy-stemmed goblets usually made from pewter or silver, although there are surviving examples made of earthenware, horn, and even glass. For your recreated feast, metal (pewter or silver) or pottery will make the best presentation. Beer was drunk from tankards, also known as jacks, made from pewter, earthenware, leather, or wood. If suggesting that your guests share a goblet seems like carrying togetherness a little too far, it is perfectly all right if everyone gets his or her own. But until well into the eleventh century, nobles and commoners alike frequently slept together on the floor of the great hall, so shared drinking vessels did not seem overly familiar to them.

Unbelievably, until well into the fourteenth century, even spoons were shared. Because only the richest households were likely to have enough spoons on hand for each guest at a large banquet, guests had to share whatever spoons were available or bring their own.

Since bringing a spoon to a feast was so common, people competed to have the grandest spoon. Some were encrusted with jewels and worn around the neck like jewelry. Whether or not spoons were provided, everyone was expected to bring a knife. Small knives were constantly worn on the belt of every medieval person, regardless of social position. These "belt knives" (not to be confused with the larger daggers) were the primary eating utensil of medieval society.

For authenticity at your medieval banquet, your guests should be required to bring their own knives and encouraged to bring their own spoons. Relate to them the above story, and suggest that people decorate their spoons to see who can achieve the most elaborate results while still being able to eat with it.

If there hasn't been any mention of medieval forks, it's because there weren't any. The fork did not become popular in most of Europe until nearly 1500, and not in England until nearly 1600. Although there were

attempts to introduce forks into northern Europe from Byzantium and Spain, where they had been widely popular for centuries, the northern Europeans thought that putting an eating utensil into the mouth was a filthy habit practiced only by barbarians.

Your table settings should begin with tablecloths; salt cellars, the grandest being at the center of the high table, more humble ones on each of the lower tables; and shared plates (for fruit and bread) and drinking vessels. Provide each individual with a soup bowl, possibly a spoon, and a cloth napkin. If you want to be truly medieval, one napkin the length of the table should be draped across the laps of an entire row of diners. Each table should be provided with several loaves of bread and bowls of butter mixed with herbs or honey (see chapter 9). Bread and butter were served as appetizers at the medieval banquet and were already on the table before the guests took their seats. Sometimes the bread and butter were augmented by a selection of cheeses.

A variety of leather, wooden, and pewter tankards, along with wooden bowls, can make even a modern table appear medieval. PHOTO BY STEVE LUND

47

SEATING AND SERVING

At the appointed signal, usually a sign from a servant, the guests all gathered at the tables and stood behind their seats. When those at the high table had seated themselves, they signaled the beginning of the feast by inviting their guests to "take their ease."

Wine, beer, and other drinks should be brought to the table first so the guests can refresh themselves. For best period effect, serve the drinks from large earthenware pitchers—which were known as flagons, jacks, or aquamanailes, depending on their size, shape, and contents—and serve all the drinks at room temperature.

Once the diners have their drinks, the next order of business is for guests to wash their hands. The most common eating utensil during the Middle Ages was the fingers, so the importance of hand washing was raised to near ritual level. Pages with pitchers, bowls, and towels moved from diner to diner, starting with the high table, allowing each guest to wash his or her

hands. Additional washings between courses were not unusual, and a final washing at the end of the meal was absolutely mandatory. The water with which guests wash should be scented with fragrant oils (a bit of mint or vanilla extract will do nicely) and decorated with rose petals or violets.

Because of the importance of religion in medieval life, it was inevitable that a short service, or at least a prayer, preceded a feast. If one of the guests at your recreated feast has come dressed as a monk or nun, having him or her read or recite the medieval Latin Pater Noster (the Lord's Prayer) would not be out of order. Below is the Pater Noster in twelfth-century church Latin. Latin is phonetic, so every letter is pronounced. For instance, each u in the word *tuum* is pronounced, making the word read "too-um." The prayer should properly be performed by making the sign of the cross in the air, with the index finger and middle finger of the right hand extended upward, at the beginning and the end of the prayer. When making the sign of the cross, say, "Et nomine patre, e et filis, e et spitirtus sancti . . ." ("In the name of the Father and of the Son and of the Holy Spirit . . .")

Pater Noster, que es in calis,
sanctificúe nomen tuum.
Adveniáte regnum tuum.
Fiat volúntas tua, sicut in caelo et in terra.
Panem nostrum cottidiánum da nobis
    hódie.
Et dimítte nobis débita nostra, sicut et nos
    dimíttimus debitóribus nostrus.
Et ne nos indúcas in tentatiónem:
sed líbera nos a malo.
Amen.

After the opening ceremonies, the time has come to serve the first course, or remove. Those at the high table are always served first, and never served from behind—the risk of assassination was too high to ever allow a server to get behind his or her lord or lady. If necessary, serve other guests from behind, but not those at the high table. Once the "nobles" have been served and the waiter moves away from the seats of honor, he must be certain not to turn his back to the hosts; in the Middle Ages, this was cause for immediate dismissal from service, or at least a good beating. If the guests are seated on only one side of the table, serving should be done from the open side of the table, but those at the seats of honor are still served first.

The traditional interval between removes is the perfect time for toasts, conversation, and songs.

Just as diners were paired to share utensils, they were also expected to assist each other in the serving process. Gentlemen served their ladies, younger diners served elder partners, and pages served their masters. Such courtesy extended to carving meat from a fowl or roast. Two fingers were used to hold the meat steady on the platter, known as a charger, while the belt knife was used to carve away pieces of meat, which were then served to the dining partner, after which the server served him or herself. Those who brought the food into the hall were never allowed to serve it.

As the courses are served, each diner should be offered a first helping by the waiter, who then places the charger on the table so that guests have an easy reach for additional helpings. The chargers can then be passed among the diners at will. At actual medieval feasts, those at the high table were routinely served better food and more courses than the rest of the guests, but this is unnecessary at a modern, recreated feast.

TABLE MANNERS

With the medieval emphasis on social position and courtliness juxtaposed with the fact that so much food was consumed with the fingers, it is easy to see that great emphasis had to be placed on good manners. Medieval etiquette dictated that "diners not spit on, nor across, the table, nor belch or break wind while seated . . . or pick your nose nor finger nails while dining."

Although food was cut both on the serving platter and on the trencher with the belt knife, under no circumstances was it put into the mouth on the end of a knife blade. Food was cut into bite-size pieces on the trencher and then eaten with the fingers, or one end of a large piece of meat could be taken into the mouth, held firmly between the teeth, and cut free just in front of the lips with the knife, the latter option being one that only men would use. For your feast, it is a lot safer for guests to cut the food on their plates and put it in their mouths with their fingers.

The broth from soups was drunk from the bowl as though it were a cup, and the solids were eaten with the fingers or a spoon. Be certain that your soup bowls do not have sloping sides or wide lips, or they will be almost impossible to drink out of.

BETWEEN REMOVES

Between courses, or removes, a short period of relaxation should take place to allow the food to settle and give diners time to excuse themselves briefly from the table, although during the Middle Ages it was considered rude to leave the table, and small containers were discreetly set beneath the table to take care of nature's call. During these idle periods, the company can exchange toasts. Toasts to the host, hostess, honored guests, the season that brought the company together, and the cooks are all in order. The company may also wish to sing songs or play some of the games designed for the dinner table (see chapters 11 and 13).

At the end of the feast, just prior to the start of the evening's main entertainment, if any is scheduled, the steward, butler, or cook presents the pièce de résistance, the grand subtlety. Subtleties are fantastical desserts made of candies, pastries, and cake. The idea is to create an edible fantasy for the entertainment of the guests. Complete directions for creating your own subtlety are given in chapter 9.

An integral part of courtly manners and religious duty was the practice of almsgiving. Alms was a polite name given to food left on the table at the end of the meal. The leftovers, including the trencher breads, were collected in a large bowl by the almoner, who was usually the household priest, monk, or chaplain, and distributed to the poor who gathered at the castle gate. While we no longer pass out leftover food to the less fortunate, you can explain the practice to the guests and have the cleric who said the prayer, or the host, pass a bowl among the guests to take up a collection to be given to a local charity. This should probably be done prior to serving the grand subtlety, so the company has not begun to break up before they have a chance to contribute. If you are holding a play (such as the version of Robyn Hode found in chapter 12) at the end of the meal, this can also be a good time to collect money for charity.

AFTER DINNER

When the feast is over and the kitchen help has cleared the table, you may need to have people help remove the tables and chairs from the feast hall to make room for any dancing, singing, or entertaining that is to take place.

CHAPTER 8
THE MENU

◆

For a period of history not usually noted for its record keeping, descriptions of medieval feasts are surprisingly numerous and detailed. From detailed shopping lists in royal budgets to fanciful accounts in such works as Chaucer's *Canterbury Tales*, food and feasts seem to have been almost as important to our medieval ancestors as were courtly love and glorious battles. The reason for this food obsession is simple: Feasts were powerful symbols of social position in a world where many, if not most, people lived on the verge of malnutrition.

The variety and elaborateness of the dishes served at medieval feasts were limited only by the wealth of the host and the creative talents of the kitchen. Generally, the higher in the social order a household was, the more the diet tended toward red meat and red wine. Vegetables were only served cooked and were usually thought to be beneath the palates of the nobility. The clergy, for reasons that are unknown, warned people against eating salads, and physicians advised against eating raw fruit.

At major feasts, every effort was made to provide the broadest variety of dishes that the season and money would allow. Holiday menus, even in midsize manor houses and small castles, could be astonishing in both abundance and complexity. Four or five courses, called removes, each containing ten to sixteen dishes, were not uncommon. When Henry IV was crowned king of England in 1399, his coronation banquet must have been impressive, even for its time. The entire meal was dutifully recorded by Jean de Froissart in his *Chronicles*.

FIRST REMOVE
Meat in pepper sauce, *Viaund Ryal* [a crustless cheese and ale quiche], Boar's head and tusks [mostly as a decoration for high table], *Grand Chare* [a meat dish], Cygnets [baby swan], Fat Capon [a type of chicken], Pheasant, Heron, Lombardy Custard [custard with dried fruit], Sturgeon, a Subtlety [an elaborate dessert].

SECOND REMOVE
Venison in frumenty [a wheat custard], Jelly [a cold, jellied meat], Stuffed Boar, Peacocks [probably redressed in their own feathers before being served], Crane, Roast Venison, Coney [rabbit], Bittern [a seabird], Pullets [half-grown hens], Great Tarts [probably a meat and fruit pie], Fried Meat, Leech Custard [date paste with wine syrup], and a Subtlety.

THIRD REMOVE
Quince in comfit [quinces probably stewed in wine], Egrets, Curlews, Partridge, Pigeons, Quails, Snipes, Small Birds, Rabbits, Glazed meat-apples [meatballs], White meat *leche* [poultry stewed in wine],

Glazed eggs [probably hard-boiled and painted with an edible glaze], Fritters [similar to doughnuts, sometimes made with ground meat in them], Doucettes [a custard and bone marrow pie], *Pety perneux* [quiche tarts with currants and dates], Eagle, *Pottys of lylye* [unknown], a Subtlety.

Feasts were intended to last throughout the day, or over the course of several days, and during those periods when food was being served, guests were expected to take only small helpings of those foods that appealed to their palates, while declining the rest. The prodigious amounts of leftovers were then offered to the servants or given to the poor as a sign of the noble lord's charity.

The feast culminated with the presentation of a grand subtlety. Subtleties were extravagant desserts such as dragons sculpted from marzipan, ships made from cake, forests of spun honey, or even four-and-twenty blackbirds slipped inside a pie shell, presented for the amusement of the guests. Ice sculptures, gingerbread houses, and scantily clad ladies jumping out of cakes are the nearest modern equivalent.

It is obvious from the menu above that not all the foods served at medieval feasts would appeal to modern appetites, nor are the ingredients readily obtainable at the local market. Therefore, the menu suggested here will be offered in three removes, followed by a grand subtlety, with a variety of options for each dish in each remove. Choose your combination of dishes in each remove carefully for balance in color, taste, and texture. Because some of the combinations of ingredients and procedures may be unfamiliar to modern cooks, it is best to try the recipes before serving them to guests. Also review the ingredients list carefully; some, like bone marrow and a few of the spices, may require

Cooking over an open fire not only adds to the medieval look of an event, but also provides the rich smell of a medieval kitchen. Photo by Robert Whitehouse

ordering ahead. If your grocer can't get some of the ingredients, check with gourmet food stores or specialty butcher shops.

Wherever possible, make the dishes ahead of time and reheat them just before serving. Bread, soup, and the grand subtlety can all be made days ahead and frozen until the day of the feast. A microwave oven can do as much work as four assistant cooks in a steamy medieval kitchen.

When preparing the dishes for delivery to the table, remember that most medieval food was never portioned onto plates. Solid foods were served on great platters called chargers, while soups were served from tureens, and guests could take as much or as little as they pleased. But caution your guests that there will be ten dishes served over the course of the meal so they don't take too much of any one thing.

If you want to let your guests know what they are going to be eating, write out the menu on the menu border in the color section of this book, have it color copied, and send it out with the invitation or information packet.

MENU

FIRST REMOVE
Bread
  select one: parsley bread
                    barley bread
Butter
  herb butter and honey butter
Cheeses
  a selection of cheeses
Soup
  select one: squash in broth
                    pea soup

SECOND REMOVE
Boar's head
  presentational, for the high table only
Fish or poultry
  select one: fruit and salmon pie
                    chicken with milk and honey
Salad
  select one: herbs with vegetables and flowers
                    compost
  (we suggest the herbed vegetables with the salmon pie and the compost with the chicken)
Side dish
  select one: lemon rice with almonds
                    herb fritters
  (we suggest the rice with the salmon pie and the fritters with the chicken)
Subtlety
  select one: pears in compost
                    cherry potage
  (we suggest the pears with the salmon and the potage with the chicken)

THIRD REMOVE
    Meat
        select one: pork in spicy syrup
                   game pie
    Vegetable
        select one: cabbage with marrow
                   Ember Day tarts
    Side dish
        select one: mushroom tarts
                   applesauce with pears
    (we suggest the tarts with the pork and the applesauce with the pie)

FOURTH REMOVE
    Grand subtlety
        select one: live frog pie
                   gingerbread castle

CHAPTER 9

RECIPES

◆

FIRST REMOVE

Bread. As an alternative to baking your own bread, you can substitute store-bought bread. We suggest buying only naturally shaped loaves rather than those baked in pans. For the high table, select a white bread like French or Italian; for those next in line, choose a light brown, whole-meal bread; and for those at the end of the hall, serve a pumpernickel or rye.

PARSLEY BREAD

2 pkgs. (½ oz.) dry yeast (active)

1¾ c. warm water

6 tbsp. honey

8 c. (or more) all-purpose unbleached white flour (not self-rising)

6 eggs

1 egg yolk

⅔ c. chopped dates or softened currants

1⅔ tbsp. salt

6 tbsp. oil

1½ tsp. rosemary

1½ tsp. basil

⅔ c. finely chopped fresh parsley

1½ tsp. cinnamon

Sprinkle yeast in ½ cup warm water and stir in the honey. Let stand for 5 minutes. Add remaining water to the yeast; beat in 3 cups of flour. Cover with damp cloth, place in a warm place, and allow to rise for 45 minutes, or until the dough doubles in size. Knead the mixture down.

Beat together 5 eggs and 1 egg yolk. Stir in the currants. Beat in the salt and oil. Mix combined ingredients into the dough.

Crush together the dried herbs and the fresh parsley. Stir in the cinnamon, and then add to the dough and beat well. If the parsley is fresh, the bread will take on a pale green color. Stir in the remaining flour a spoonful at a time, until the dough comes away from the side of the bowl.

Place the dough onto a lightly floured work surface, and knead until the dough is smooth and elastic, about 10 to 12 minutes, adding the occasional sprinkle of flour if necessary.

Clean out the mixing bowl and grease the sides. Return the dough to the bowl, cover with a damp cloth, and set in a warm place until it doubles in size, about 1 hour. For a finer-textured bread, give the dough an additional kneading and rising.

Knead down the dough, and place it on a greased cookie sheet. Cover with a damp towel, and set in a warm place to rise until doubled in size, about a half hour.

During the final rise, preheat the oven to 425° F. When the bread has risen, beat the remaining egg white and brush it on the surface of the loaf. Bake the loaf for 45 to 50 minutes, or until the surface is nicely brown and the crust sounds solid when tapped. Remove from oven and cool. Can be made ahead. Each loaf serves 6 to 8. (Adapted from *Fabulous Feasts*.)

BARLEY BREAD

1 lb. 3 oz. whole-meal flour

8 oz. barley flour

½ tsp. salt

2 pkgs. (½ oz.) dry yeast (active)

⅓ c. dark brown ale

2 c. warm water

2 tsp. honey

Mix the dry ingredients in a bowl and set aside. Mix the yeast and a little brown ale until it becomes creamy, then add 1½ cups water and the honey to the yeast mixture. Set aside for 5 minutes.

Stir the yeast mixture into the dry ingredients until it forms a firm dough, adding a little extra water if needed. Place the dough onto a lightly floured work surface, and knead until the dough is smooth and elastic, about 10 to 12 minutes, adding the occasional sprinkle of flour if necessary.

Clean out the mixing bowl and grease the sides. Return the dough to the bowl, cover with a damp cloth, and set in a warm place until it doubles in size, about 1 hour. For a finer-textured bread, give the dough an additional kneading and rising.

Divide the dough into two round loaves, place them on greased cookie sheets, cover with a damp towel, and set in a warm place to rise until doubled in size, about a half hour.

During the final rise, preheat the oven to 425° F. Bake the loaf for 45 to 50 minutes, or until the surface is nicely brown and the crust sounds solid when tapped. Remove from oven and cool. Can be made ahead. Makes 2 loaves. Each loaf serves 6 to 8. (Adapted from various sources, as found in *The Medieval Cookbook*.)

HONEY BUTTER

1 lb. butter

⅓ c. honey

Allow the butter to come to room temperature. Blend the butter and honey together thoroughly. Shape into a mound or spoon into small cups. Chill before serving. Can be made ahead. One batch serves 12 to 14.

HERB BUTTER

1 lb. butter

¼ c. dried herbs or ½ c. finely chopped fresh herbs (equal parts basil, thyme, and parsley)

Allow the butter to come to room temperature. Blend the butter and herbs together thoroughly. Shape into a mound or spoon into small cups. Chill before serving. If you are using dried herbs, allow at least 8 hours for the herbs to soften in the butter before serving. Can be made ahead. One batch serves 12 to 14.

CHEESES

Serve a nice selection of both hard and soft cheeses. We suggest such soft cheeses as Brie and Camembert and such traditional hard cheeses as Cheddar and Stilton. If possible, place large wedges or entire small wheels of cheese on a large platter to allow guests to serve themselves. Can be prepared ahead.

Squash in Broth

2 lbs. pumpkin or butternut squash

4 to 6 c. beef, pork, vegetable, or chicken stock (bouillon can be substituted)

3 to 4 onions, minced

½ lb. ground pork

1 tbsp. brown sugar

2 tbsp. minced parsley

½ tsp. salt

¼ tsp. ginger

¼ tsp. cinnamon

⅛ tsp. nutmeg

Skin, seed, and cube the squash; set aside. Brown the pork and onion, with salt, in a skillet. Drain off the fat. Place the stock in a soup kettle, and add pork and onions, squash, spices, brown sugar, and parsley. Simmer covered about 10 minutes, until squash is tender but still firm. Serve hot. Can be made ahead, frozen, and reheated. If you plan to freeze this, slightly undercook it so the squash will not become mushy when it is reheated. Serves 8 to 10. (Adapted from *Two Fifteenth Century Cookery Books*, as translated in *To the King's Taste* and *The Forme of Cury*, as found in *Pleyn Delit*.)

Pea Soup

3 lbs. green peas, fresh or frozen

4 c. vegetable stock or bouillon

3 onions, peeled and minced

1 tbsp. brown sugar

½ tsp. salt

½ tsp. saffron

fresh, coarsely ground pepper

Bring stock to boil in large saucepan or kettle. Add remaining ingredients to the broth, cover, and simmer 15 minutes or until peas are quite soft. Puree the soup in a blender. Return the soup to the pot and reheat. Garnish with pepper. Can be made well ahead, frozen, and reheated. Serves 6 to 8. (Adapted from *Curye on Inglysch*, as found in *The Medieval Cookbook* and *Two Fifteenth Century Cookery Books*, as translated in *To the King's Taste*.)

SECOND REMOVE

BOAR'S HEAD

Arrange with your butcher to get the head of a pig from the slaughterhouse. When the head arrives, trim any loose flesh from around the base of the head. Preheat the oven to 350° F. Pry open the mouth, and wedge in a firm, red apple. Place the head in a large baking pan and roast it, uncovered, until it turns golden brown. For an added sheen, brush the head several times with a beaten egg during the last half hour it is in the oven. Place on a platter, garnish with greens, and serve to the high table. Can be made ahead and frozen until the day before it is needed.

FRUIT AND SALMON PIE

1 lb. cooked salmon cut into 1-inch pieces, or a similar amount of canned salmon, flaked

½ lemon

1 c. sweet red wine

1 c. figs, chopped

½ c. dates, pitted and quartered

¼ c. raisins

¼ c. currants

1½ tbsp. pine nuts

½ tsp. ground cinnamon

¼ tsp. pepper

¼ tsp. ground cloves

¼ tsp. salt

⅛ tsp. mace

⅛ tsp. ground ginger

1 unbaked 9-inch pastry shell and top crust

Glaze

2 tbsp. milk

¼ tsp. pulverized almonds

⅛ tsp. saffron

Preheat oven to 375° F. Place the salmon in a bowl, squeeze on the lemon, and stir to distribute evenly on the fish; set aside. Simmer the figs in wine for 10 minutes, or until soft. Remove figs and place in a mixing bowl. In the same wine, simmer the dates for three minutes, then remove dates to a separate bowl.

To the figs, add all of the spices except the pine nuts. Add the raisins and currants and mix well. Spread this mixture in the bottom of the pie shell, and sprinkle the pine nuts across the mixture. Alternate the salmon and dates on the surface of the pie. Close the pie with a top crust, and crimp the edges. Pierce the lid with a fork, and make a small vent hole in the center. Combine the ingredients for the glaze, and brush on the surface of the pie. Bake 35 to 40 minutes or until well browned. Each pie serves 6 to 8. (Adapted from *Fabulous Feasts*.)

CHICKEN WITH MILK AND HONEY

3- to 4-lb. chicken, cut into pieces

3 c. milk

½ c. flour mixed with ½ tsp. salt and ⅛ tsp. pepper

⅓ c. honey

⅓ c. pine nuts

3 tbsp. oil

3 tbsp. minced parsley

2 tbsp. chopped mint

1 tsp. vinegar

⅛ tsp. rubbed sage

½ tsp. savory

½ tsp. saffron

½ tsp. salt

¼ tsp. pepper

Dredge the chicken pieces in the flour. Brown the chicken in oil in a large skillet until golden. Mix milk, honey, herbs, salt, and pepper in a bowl. Pour the mixture over the browned chicken. Stir to combine the mixture with the natural juices of the chicken. Cover and simmer about 30 minutes, or until the chicken is tender. Stir in the pine nuts just before serving. Serves 6. (Adapted from *Two Fifteenth Century Cookery Books*, as translated in *To the King's Taste*.)

Herbs With Vegetables

4 c. fresh chopped parsley

1 c. chopped watercress

1 c. leeks, finely chopped

½ c. fresh chopped sage

½ c. chopped onion

3 cloves garlic, finely chopped

6 sprigs mint, finely chopped

¼ c. olive oil

½ c. wine vinegar

salt to taste

Mix the ingredients together in a bowl, and toss them with the oil. Serve and sprinkle with vinegar and salt. Can be made several hours beforehand. Serves 6. (Adapted from *Two Fifteenth Century Cookery Books*, as translated in *To the King's Taste*.)

Compost

¼ head (about 1 lb.) cabbage, coarsely shredded

4 parsnips, peeled and cubed

4 carrots, peeled and cubed

3 turnips, peeled and cubed

2 hard pears, peeled, cored, and cubed

2 c. muscatel (sweet white wine)

2 c. white wine vinegar

¼ c. currants or raisins

6 tbsp. sugar

4 tbsp. honey

4 tbsp. salt

½ tsp. cinnamon

½ tsp. whole cloves

½ tsp each coarsely crushed aniseed and mustard seed

¼ tsp. saffron

¼ tsp. pepper

¼ tsp. allspice

Add salt to 2 quarts water and bring to a boil in a 6-quart kettle. Add the vegetables and return the water to boiling. Reduce heat to simmer, cover, and cook for 5 to 7 minutes. Add the pears and cook an additional 10 minutes, until all ingredients are tender but still firm. Drain, place the vegetables and pears in a large mixing bowl, and set aside.

In a saucepan, combine wine, vinegar, sugar, and honey. Heat until bubbly. Add saffron and cinnamon, stirring until well blended. Pour the syrup over the vegetables, stirring until they are well coated. Place the remaining spices in a square of lightweight cloth, and tie it shut with a piece of string. Drop the pickling spices into the compost mixture. Add currants or raisins and stir the mixture well. Place the kettle in the refrigerator overnight. Remove the spice bag before serving. Can be served cold or warmed. Can be made well ahead and stored in the refrigerator or canned. Serves 12 to 14. (Adapted from *Curye on Inglysch*, as found in *The Medieval Cookbook* and *Two Fifteenth Century Cookery Books*, as translated in *To the King's Taste*.)

Lemon Rice With Almonds

2 lemons

4 c. water

2 c. uncooked white rice

2 c. dry white wine

2 c. fresh (or frozen) peas

1⅓ c. currants

1⅓ c. coarsely ground almonds

⅔ c. honey

2 tbsp. butter or margarine

1 tsp. cinnamon

1 tsp. salt

Grate the zest from the lemons. Squeeze the lemons, reserving the juice and pulp. Discard the membranes and seeds. In a large saucepan, bring the water, rice, salt, cinnamon, butter, and lemon juice, pulp, and zest to a boil. Reduce to simmer, cover, and cook until the water has been absorbed, about 15 minutes. Stir once during the simmering process. Add the peas to the rice for the last 7 minutes.

While the rice is cooking, simmer the almonds and currants in the wine for 7 or 8 minutes. When the rice is cooked, remove from the fire, and fluff with a fork, adding the wined almonds and currants as you stir. Dribble the honey on the surface of the dish just before serving. Serves 6. (Adapted from *Fabulous Feasts*.)

Herb Fritters

4 c. flour

3 c. lukewarm water

1 c. finely chopped fresh herbs, such as parsley, savory, sage, marjoram, chives, rosemary

2 pkgs. (½ oz.) dry yeast (active)

1 tsp. salt

frying oil

honey to garnish

Dissolve the yeast in 1 cup warm water. In a bowl, mix together the flour, herbs, and salt. Stir the yeast water into the mixture, and add enough water to make a smooth, thick batter. Stir until free of lumps. Cover the batter and let rise for 1 hour. Heat the frying oil. Drop the batter into the hot oil a large spoonful at a time. If you are not deep frying the fritters, turn them once. Serve and garnish with honey. Makes 20 to 24 golf-ball-size fritters. (Adapted from *The Forme of Cury*, as found in *Pleyn Delit*.)

Pears in Compost

6 large, ripe, sweet pears

3 c. malmsey (heavy, sweet red wine)

¾ c. sliced dates

3 tbsp. sugar

1½ tbsp. cinnamon

¼ tsp. ginger

dash salt

Peel, pare, and quarter the pears. Parboil until they begin to turn tender; do not let them get soft. Drain. In a large saucepan, heat wine, cinnamon, ginger, and sugar. When the mixture is hot, add the dates, pears, and salt. Bring to a boil, lower heat to simmer, and cook for 8 to 10 minutes. Allow to cool slightly before serving. Can be made a day ahead and reheated. Serves 6. (Adapted from *Two Fifteenth Century Cookery Books*, as found in *Recipes for Æthelmearc 12th Night*.)

Cherry Potage

2 lbs. ripe, red cherries

1½ c. light, sweet red wine

¾ c. sugar

4 tbsp. unsalted butter

2½ c. soft, white bread crumbs

⅛ tsp. salt

Wash the cherries and remove the stems and pits. Puree with a mixer or in a blender, along with 10 tablespoons of the wine and half of the sugar. If necessary, add a little more wine. In a saucepan, melt the butter and add the fruit puree, bread crumbs, remaining wine, sugar, and salt. Simmer slowly, stirring constantly, until the mixture is very thick. Pour into a serving bowl, cover, and place in the refrigerator to cool. Just before serving, you may decorate the edge of the bowl with small, fresh flowers or spoonfuls of thick whipped cream. Can be made one or two days ahead. Serves 8. (Adapted from *Curye on Inglysch*, as found in *The Medieval Cookbook*.)

THIRD REMOVE
Pork in Spicy Syrup

4-lb. pork roast with bone

2 c. malmsey or other heavy, sweet red wine

4 tbsp. cooking oil or butter

½ c. currants

¾ c. vinegar

¾ c. sugar

2 onions, finely chopped

¾ tsp. coarsely ground black pepper

1 tsp. ground caraway seeds

1 clove garlic, crushed (optional)

1 c. chicken stock or bouillon

Remove the skin from the pork roast, and prick the fat layer, all over, with a sharp knife or large serving fork. Sauté the onions and currants in the oil. When the onions have become transparent, remove from the fire and add the wine, vinegar, sugar, spices, garlic, stock, and seasonings. Place the pork roast in a covered stew pot and spoon the marinade over it. Cover the pot, and place it in the refrigerator for 6 to 8 hours, turning the roast and spooning the marinade over it every 1½ to 2 hours.

Preheat oven to 425° F. Cover the roast and place it in the oven, allowing 30 to 35 minutes per pound. During the last hour of cooking, remove the lid, spoon additional marinade over the roast, and return to the oven uncovered to allow the roast to brown. Remove the roast to a serving platter and pour the remaining marinade into a pitcher. Serves 8. (Adapted from *Curye on Inglysch,* as found in *The Medieval Cookbook.*)

GAME PIES

1- to 1½-lb. rabbit, jointed

1 to 1½- lb. chicken pieces

1 lb. bacon

4 ribs celery, finely chopped

4 onions, finely chopped

¼ c. butter

8 egg yolks

2 egg whites, beaten until liquid

½ c. honey

½ c. applesauce

1 c. chicken stock or bouillon

2 tbsp. chopped parsley

2 tbsp. cornstarch

1 tsp. salt

½ tsp. pepper

½ tsp. grated nutmeg

½ tsp. cinnamon

2 9-inch pastry shells and top crusts

Parboil the chicken and rabbit for 15 minutes. Remove from water and allow to cool. Cut into 1-inch-square chunks, removing the skin from the chicken. Fry the bacon, and cut into ½-inch-long strips. Sauté the onions and celery in the bacon drippings until the onion is soft (add a little oil if necessary). Drain the onion and celery, and mix with the cubed meat.

Add the cornstarch to the chicken stock, seal tightly in a jar, and shake vigorously until well mixed. Place in a small saucepan and heat until slightly thickened, stirring constantly. Mix in the remaining ingredients, except the egg white; set aside.

Preheat oven to 425° F. Brush the inside of the pastry crust with some of the egg white. Place the meat, onion, and celery mixture into the crusts.

Pour the stock mixture over the meat and vegetables, crimp the lid securely into place, coat with remaining egg white, and pierce the lid with a knife in four or five places.

Bake for 15 to 20 minutes at 425°, then reduce the heat to 350° and bake for 40 to 45 minutes longer, until the crust is golden brown. May be served hot or cold. Can be made one day ahead. Makes 2 pies. Each pie serves 6 to 8. (Adapted from *Two Fifteenth Century Cookery Books,* as found in *The Medieval Cookbook,* and from *Warwickshire Country Recipes.*)

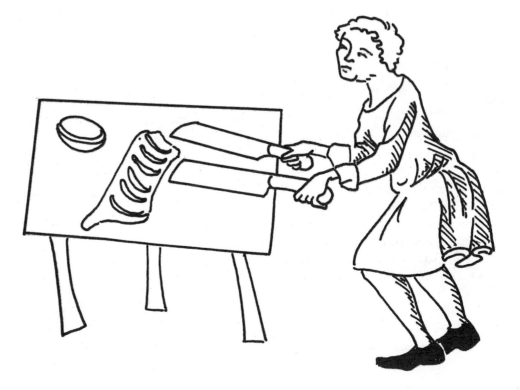

Cabbage With Marrow

8 marrow bones split lengthwise

5 c. beef broth or bouillon

1 medium head of cabbage

2 c. bread crumbs

2 tsp. salt

½ tsp. saffron

½ tsp. thyme

Boil marrow bones in beef broth until the marrow is soft, about 30 minutes. Skim the grease from the broth, remove the bones, and set the broth aside. Remove the marrow from the bones, coarsely chop the marrow, and set it aside. Wash the cabbage and chop coarsely. Add the cabbage to the broth, bring to a boil, and simmer for 10 minutes. Combine the spices with the bread crumbs and the marrow, and add to the cabbage. Stir together and simmer gently for 5 to 10 minutes. Serve in a large bowl with plenty of the broth. Serves 6 to 8. (Adapted from *Two Fifteenth Century Cookery Books*, as translated in *Take a Thousand Eggs or More*, Vol. I, and *Fabulous Feasts*.)

Ember Day Tarts

3 large or 4 medium onions, chopped

2 bunches parsley, chopped

4 eggs

½ c. cottage cheese

¼ c. sage leaves, chopped

3 tbsp. bread crumbs

3 tbsp. currants

2 tbsp. melted butter

½ tsp. salt

¼ tsp. sugar

⅛ tsp. powdered cloves

⅛ tsp. powdered mace

⅛ tsp. saffron

1 9-inch pie shell (no top crust)

Preheat oven to 375° F. Parboil the onions and herbs, drain well, add to melted butter. Blend the cottage cheese with the eggs. Add the cheese and egg mixture to the onions and herbs. Add remaining ingredients and pour into the pie shell. Bake for about 45 minutes, or until a toothpick inserted into the custard comes out clean and the crust is golden brown. Makes 2 tarts. Each tart serves 6 to 8. (Adapted from *Forme of Curye*, as found in *Pleyn Delit*.)

Mushroom Tarts

1½ lbs. button mushrooms, sliced thin

½ c. grated mild cheddar cheese

¼ c. butter

2 tbsp. olive oil

½ tsp. salt

½ tsp. ginger

¼ tsp. pepper

1 9-inch pastry shell with top crust

Preheat oven to 375° F. Sauté the mushrooms in the butter; drain. Into the mushrooms, mix the oil, cheese, and spices. Pour the mixture in the pie shell, add the top crust, and crimp into place. Pierce with a knife in four or five places. Bake for 40 minutes, until pastry is golden brown. Makes 2 tarts. Each tart serves 6 to 8. (Adapted from *Le Menagier de Paris*, as found in *Recipes for Æthelmearc 12th Night*.)

Applesauce With Pears

4 cooking apples

3 hard pears

1 tbsp. cornstarch

½ c. sweet white wine

¼ c. raisins

¼ c. shredded almonds

¼ cup dates, finely chopped

3 tbsp. honey

2 tbsp. sugar

¼ tsp. cinnamon

⅛ tsp. ginger

Peel and core the apples, and parboil until they are soft. Remove from the stove and mash finely. Mix the white wine and cornstarch in a jar with a tight-fitting lid and shake vigorously till blended. Add the wine mixture to the pulverized apples, add the remaining ingredients except the pears, and cook till mixture begins to thicken. Remove from heat. Peel and core the pears, and parboil until they begin to soften. When they have cooled, cut into ½-inch squares. Mix the pears with the applesauce. May be reheated before serving or served chilled. Can be made several days ahead, longer if frozen. Serves 6 to 8. (Adapted from *Two Fifteenth Century Cookery Books*, as found in *Take a Thousand Eggs or More*, Vol. II.)

FOURTH REMOVE
LIVE FROG PIE

Serves no one but is a lot of fun. This is a variation on the four-and-twenty-blackbird pie mentioned in the nursery rhyme, in which candy is substituted for the family canary.

top and bottom pie crusts to fit pan as described below

dried beans or peas, enough to fill the pie shell

2 egg yolks

½ tsp. cinnamon

3 to 4 lbs. brightly wrapped candy, cheap jewelry, and other "treasures" as necessary to fill the pie

Preheat oven to 425° F. Make a pie shell and lid to fit the largest baking dish you can find; even a turkey roasting pan isn't too big. When rolling out the dough, make it 50 percent thicker than normal. It's best to use a springform pan, so you can get the crust out of the pan without breaking it, or a cheap, disposable aluminum pan that you can cut through.

Lightly grease the pie pan and dust with flour. Press the bottom crust into the pan. Fill the pie shell with the dried beans, apply the top crust, and crimp the crusts together. Glaze with the egg yolk mixed with cinnamon. Bake 40 to 45 minutes, or until golden brown.

When the pie is cool, carefully remove from the pan. Cut a hole in the bottom of the crust and allow the beans to spill out. With a disposable aluminum pan, the crust does not have to be removed from the pan; simply cut a hole in the bottom right through the pan. Carefully insert the candy and treasures into the pie shell. Slide the finished shell onto a large, decorative platter or silver tray.

Present the pie to the high table, without letting on that it's not a real pie, and allow a special guest to cut it. After the truth is revealed, pass the subtlety around for everyone to help themselves to the candy and treasures.

GINGERBREAD CASTLE

The gingerbread house, still popular at the holidays, can easily be converted into a medieval subtlety. We have redesigned the gingerbread house into a castle. Although there was a medieval gingerbread, our recipe is not authentic. Medieval gingerbread is too soft to be shaped without falling apart. Even this modern gingerbread recipe is a little crumbly, so be careful when assembling the castle.

2 c. molasses

1½ c. shortening

12 tbsp. packed brown sugar

7½ c. whole wheat flour

3 tsp. salt

1½ tsp. baking soda

1½ tsp. ground cinnamon

1½ tsp. ground ginger

1½ tsp. ground cloves

½ tsp. ground nutmeg

½ tsp. ground allspice

Mix molasses, shortening and brown sugar. Mix in remaining ingredients. Cover and refrigerate at least 4 hours.

Preheat oven to 375° F. Roll out dough on floured board to about ⅜ inch thick. Cut 4 pieces 12½" x 5½" and 4 pieces 10" x 4". Wrap the 12½" x 5½" pieces around four Quaker Oatmeal or Mother's Oats containers (or four 7-inch-long sections of mailing tube, 4 inches in diameter), covered with greaseproof, nonstick baking paper. The remaining pieces should be placed on cookie sheets. Bake until light brown, about 10 to 12 minutes.

Carefully remove the wall sections from their trays, and if possible pull the tubes out of the towers. Assemble the towers and walls on a large tray or piece of plywood covered with aluminum foil, carefully trimming the ends of the wall sections to fit snugly against the sides of the tower. The walls can be glued to the tower with cake frosting to form a square castle with four corner towers.

Let the frosting set for an hour or so. Then, around the outside of the castle walls, make a moat of blue frosting or aluminum foil, and provide access over it with a drawbridge made of Popsicle sticks or paper. Inside the castle and beyond the moat, use green icing sprinkled with shredded coconut dyed green or green sugar to create grass. Miniature plastic knights in armor spray-painted silver will add life to the scene. A plastic *Tyrannosaurus rex* dinosaur with paper wings glued to its back makes a suitable dragon. (Adapted from *Betty Crocker's Cookbook, 1981.*)

CHAPTER 10
DRINKS AND THIRST SLAKERS

◆

Medieval people enjoyed a wide variety of beverages with and between meals; most were alcohol based. Although little was known about basic hygiene, everyone knew that drinking water was likely to make you sick. Considering that slaughterhouses, toilets, and tanneries all dumped their waste into the same rivers in which people washed, the belief that water was dangerous was more than justified.

Understandably, what people drank was largely dependent on their social and economic position. The rich drank wine. The middle class drank wine when they could afford it, but along with the poor, they subsisted on ale (beer without hops) and cider. But by and large, everyone drank. We have included a few recipes for nonalcoholic drinks to add variety and sobriety to the largely alcoholic medieval cellar of thirst slakers.

WINES
Medieval wines were generally heavier and much sweeter than most modern palates are accustomed to. The additional sugar content in medieval wines allowed them to last longer before turning to vinegar. We have tried to select a representative variety of modern wines that come close to the qualities of medieval wine, without having a great amount of dregs or being too heavy for the modern palate.

Malmsey is a very sweet, dark brown wine that is still readily available in any good wine shop at a reasonable price.

Muscatel is a very sweet white wine. The best muscatel today comes from Spain and is often labeled as Moscatel. Because it is no longer a major mover on the world market, muscatel is quite inexpensive.

The red wines of the Burgundy region of France were highly prized during the Middle Ages, and many are still highly thought of. Today many different kinds of burgundies are being produced, many of them made outside of France and reasonably priced. Two of the more authentic are Pinot Noir and Gamay. Any domestic burgundy-type wine, as long as it is not dry, will be a reasonable facsimile of medieval burgundy.

During the Middle Ages, specialty wines were made from a staggering variety of fruits, flowers, berries, herbs, and vegetables. These included violet, lavender, sage, mint, strawberry, gooseberry, raisin, rhubarb, rose, currant, damson, birch, turnip, parsnip, blackberry, cherry, elderberry, wormwood, rose, apple, and balm. Some of these are still made by small wineries and can be found in specialty wine shops.

If your feast is being run on a tight budget, consider picking up a readily available Kosher wine such as Manechewitz. Because they are quite sweet, full-bodied, and come in a variety of grape and berry flavors, they are good substitutes for medieval wines. Whatever wines you choose to use with your medieval feast, be careful that they are not sparkling, or bubbly wines.

BEER AND ALE

All medieval beer was actually ale; that is to say that it was made without hops, which gives modern beer its distinctive bitter taste. Because medieval ale was poured directly from a wooden cask, it was also still, which means that it did not have the foamy head most of us are accustomed to seeing on a good beer. Like medieval wines, much of the ale of the time was heavy with sediment. All medieval ale had far more body than modern lagers and would therefore be more full-bodied than most American drinkers are used to. The closest that you are likely to come to medieval ale, without making it yourself, is modern English bitter or stout. Some of the brands most commonly found in the United States include McEwans, Samuel Smiths, Theakstons, Speckled Hen, John Smiths, and Guinness. There are also a wide variety of small brewery bitter beers that are occasionally available.

For a more medieval look and taste to your ale, try to purchase a small keg. Allow the keg to rest after transporting it, and serve it with a tap rather than a pump. To use a tap, the keg will have to be placed on its side rather than the usual vertical position. This will allow the beer to be nearly still. We also recommend that it not be chilled before serving. All medieval ale was served at room temperature, because there was no way of keeping it cold, and even modern English beer is designed to taste best if only slightly cool, not cold, the way American beer is usually served.

MEAD

Often thought of as a Viking drink, mead was popular, if rare. Mead is wine brewed with honey, the only natural sweetener commonly available in the Middle Ages. Some specialty wine shops still have mead, or can get it, but it may be expensive for the table, especially for a company of hearty drinkers. We suggest serving it as an appetizer or an aperitif.

HARD CIDER

The Normans supposedly introduced cider to England shortly after their conquest of 1066, and although it has remained popular there ever since, hard cider has, until recently, been almost impossible to find in the United States. Now, however, there are several brands being exported to America, and a few domestic brands are coming onto the market. These should be available through a good beer distributor or in a wine store. This is not the ordinary apple cider Americans buy around Halloween time; it is a fermented drink with a 6 to 8 percent alcohol content, making it stronger than any beer. When buying hard cider, choose a sweet, rather than a dry, to make it more authentically medieval.

ALTERNATIVES

If you are dedicated to putting on an authentically medieval feast and have some extra time on your hands, you might want to consider brewing your own ale, mead, or wine. The most accessible and most authentically medieval recipe book for brewing is unquestionably *A Sip through Time*, by Cindy Renfrow. You should be able to order it through your local bookstore by giving them the ISBN number 0-9628598-3-4.

PUNCHES AND MIXED DRINKS

Wines could not be aged during the Middle Ages and started to turn sour over the course of eight or ten months. Consequently, people doctored old wine to make it more palatable. Some of these concoctions became very popular, particularly around the holiday season. The wassail drink that is sung about in the Christmas carol is most likely the one described below. Any of the recipes can be increased to make as much of the drink as desired.

HIPPOCRAS

8 oz. sugar

2 quarts red wine

1 tbsp. ground cinnamon

¾ tbsp. ground ginger

1 tsp. ground cloves

1 tsp. grated nutmeg

1 tsp. coarsely ground black pepper

Mix spices together and set aside. Warm the wine until it begins to steam, add sugar and stir until it is dissolved. Add the spices and allow to simmer for 10 minutes. Pour the mixture through a mesh cloth to remove the dregs of spice (an old piece of sheet or a pillowcase will do). Pour into a punch bowl and serve.

WASSAIL

Wassail was a traditional winter drink used for toasting during the holiday period. The drink is served hot, in a wooden bowl that is passed from person to person. As the bowl is passed, the person passing the bowl declares "wass hail" ("good health" in Anglo-Saxon). The recipient responds with "drink hail" ("drink to health"). Customarily, the passing of the bowl is accompanied by a kiss. The recipient takes a drink and passes the bowl to the next person, repeating the salute, and so on through the company. Our wassail recipe makes enough for about eight people.

1½ quarts sweet hard cider (you may substitute half medium dry white wine and half American sweet cider if you can't find English cider)

1 cooking apple

¼ c. butter

2 sticks cinnamon, broken into ½-inch-long pieces

2 tbsp. sugar

1 tbsp. ground cinnamon

1 tsp. whole cloves

2 chopped nutmegs or ½ tsp. ground nutmeg

Heat the cider in a saucepan till it simmers. Place the spices in a small square of cloth, and tie it shut to form a bag. Drop the spice bag into the simmering cider.

Slice the apple into ¼-inch-thick rings, removing the core but leaving the skin in place. Mix the sugar and ground cinnamon in a small bowl. Coat the apple rings with the sugar-and-cinnamon mixture. Melt the butter in a skillet; when it is hot, sauté the coated apple rings until they begin to soften. Remove the spice bag from the cider, and pour the cider into a wooden bowl. Pour the sautéed apples, along with the butter, into the hot cider. Serve.

CAUDLE

6 egg yolks

3 quarts ale (if using modern beer, let it go flat before making the caudle)

8 tbsp. sugar

½ tsp. saffron

½ tsp. salt

Beat the egg yolks until they begin to thicken. In a saucepan, warm the ale, sugar, saffron, and salt until lukewarm. Remove a cup or so of the ale, and stir it into the beaten egg yolks. Add the egg and ale mixture to the rest of the lukewarm ale. Raise the heat slightly, stirring the mixture continually until it begins to thicken. Do not allow the mixture to boil, or it will become lumpy. The finished caudle is best served immediately.

NONALCOHOLIC DRINKS

There were a few nonalcoholic drinks popularly consumed during the Middle Ages. They were not overly common, because people depended on the natural sugars in wines, meads, and ales as an important part of their diet.

MILK

Milk, then as now, was served to children, but it was often cut with "small," or weak, ale.

TEA

Tea was made by immersing fresh mint in boiling water. It takes about 2 dozen 12- to 14-inch-long sprigs of mint to a gallon of water to make a properly tasty tea. The tea was often sweetened with honey, although sugar could just as easily be used. Occasionally, a few tablespoons of vinegar were added to unsweetened mint tea to give it a distinctive tang. Vinegar in mint tea may sound odd, but it is actually quite tasty.

BERRY DRINKS

All manner of berries were used to make fresh, tasty summertime drinks. Berry juice, water, and honey or sugar might be combined to suit personal taste. Other times, berry juice was added to white wines to make them lighter, fresher, and add variety to an otherwise limited drink selection.

CHAPTER 11
GAMES AND PASTIMES

In a world where television, radio, and Nintendo games did not exist, and even literacy was a rarity, playing simple games had a far greater appeal than today. If you can get the guests at your medieval feast into the spirit of things, you and they will be amazed at how much fun they can have playing these games. Most of the games are presented here in their original form; some of them will be familiar, some pretty strange. Others are adaptations of medieval sports that are simply not practical in the modern world; in some instances, the facilities do not exist in most people's worlds, and in others, we simply feel that the premium on life is higher than it was eight centuries ago.

Because some of these games must be played outdoors, and many of those require some work to prepare, your final selection of entertainment will depend on the time of year you plan to hold your feast, the number of people that will be in attendance, and the space available. If you plan to host a Christmas celebration, it might be worth considering appointing a Lord of Misrule to help you plan the day's games and activities. It would then be his responsibility to see to it that everyone is kept busy and involved in the activities, and that all the games start at the appointed time and place. This will allow you, the hosts, to enjoy some of the party yourselves and still have time to take care of the many details that you cannot avoid. Whichever

pastimes you select, we hope you'll be amazed at the appeal still present in these simple pleasures.

BOARD GAMES

Chess. Although the rules for chess are far too extensive to provide here, suffice it to say that chess dates at least to ancient Egypt. The game as we know it was played by the Vikings in the tenth century, and written rules for the game survive from the late thirteenth century. Certainly chess was one of the most popular board games of the Middle Ages.

Predominantly played by the noble classes, chess was used as a training ground for the strategy, tactics, and thought processes that were employed in besieging castles during times of war. The relative number of pieces accurately reflects the makeup of medieval armies and society at large. There are only one king and queen, supported by a small number of clergymen (bishops), mounted warriors (knights), and castles (rooks). The bulk of the army is then made up of conscripted peasant forces (pawns), who are thrown at the enemy before the elite troops are committed to battle.

Draughts, or Checkers. Identical to the modern game, draughts, or checkers, was common during the Middle Ages. Then, however, it was more popular among women and the lower social orders who did not

Merrills. Also called Nine Man's Morris, Merrills, or variations thereof, is extremely old, certainly dating to the early Middle Ages. The accompanying illustration shows the layout of the board, and below are the rules. Markers can be small stones, coins, or any other small movable object. Most surviving boards tend to be about eight inches square, but the size varies from four and a half to ten inches square. For instructions on how to reproduce an actual medieval Merrills board, see *Medieval Furniture: Plans and Instructions for Authentic Reproductions,* by Daniel Diehl and Mark Donnelly (Stackpole Books, 1999).

understand the complex rules of chess or, in the case of women, because it was not considered as warlike as chess. The game was far more popular on the continent than it was in England, where it did not take hold until the late sixteenth or early seventeenth century.

Tables. Very much like the modern game of backgammon, tables was enjoyed by both sexes—anyone who could afford a board and marker pieces could play. The rules of tables are similar enough to backgammon that the use of a backgammon board at a recreated medieval feast would not be at all out of place.

Rules for Merrills (according to the Ryedale Folk Museum, North Yorkshire County, England, organizers of the annual World Championship Merrills Tournament):

The Board has three concentric squares linked through the center point of each side. This provides 24 intersection points arranged in 16 lines of three, on which the pieces are placed.

The Play is divided into three stages but the object throughout is to get three pieces in a line; this is called a "mill." On forming a mill, one of the opponent's pieces is removed from the board. The game is won by the player who reduces an opponent's pieces to only two, or blocks them from moving in the middle stage of the game.

The Opening stage of the game begins with an empty board. Each player, in turn, places one piece on any vacant point on the board, until both players have played all nine pieces. If either player makes a mill, that player removes any one of the opponent's pieces, providing that piece is not itself part of a mill. Throughout the game, pieces forming a mill are safe from capture. Once a piece is removed from the board it takes no further part in the game.

Note: moves and lines of three can only be made along the horizontal and vertical lines on the board, never across the diagonals, where no lines are marked.

The Middle Stage of the game commences when all the pieces are on the board, except those lost in play. Play continues alternately; each player moves one piece to any empty adjacent point, again with the object of forming a mill and removing one of the opponent's pieces. Once a mill has been formed it can be "opened" by moving one piece from the line if there is an empty point next to it and

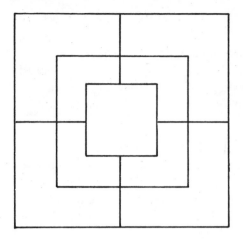

but who doesn't like chocolates), a cheap ring, a small piece of medieval-looking jewelry, or some other such token. The forfeits come in the form of demands to perform some slightly embarrassing act, such as singing a song, reciting a poem (which may or may not be included in the parcel), or juggling several pieces of fruit taken from the table. At the center of the parcel is a slightly better prize that will be the reward for the last person to receive the parcel. When you make up the parcel, be sure that there are enough layers to allow each guest to have several prizes or forfeits. If you are hosting a large banquet, you may wish to have more than one parcel made up. With slightly different prizes and forfeits, this can make a wonderful children's game.

COURT OF LOVE

Another entertainment that can be played at the feast table is performing a "court of love." Ladies may command that their gentlemen make a declaration of their undying love that must convince the assembled guests of their sincerity. This may take the form of a poem, a courtroomlike argument, or a direct plea to the lady. The presentation may be lighthearted or serious, but never demanding or nasty. Unattached gentlemen may also make declarations of their affections to unattached female members of the company. The reaction of the company, either approval or disapproval, will determine the future of the couple's relationship. Such courts of love were particularly popular during the twelfth and thirteenth centuries and probably originated in France. The first recorded courts of love were chronicled by Andreas Capellanus, chaplain to Christine de Pisan.

Since many consider love to be a sort of a game, and certainly the medieval concept of courtly love fell into this category, then like any game, love must have its rules. The following rules of love are, not surprisingly, adapted from Christine de Pisan. Some of these rules are amazingly sensible and ring true after seven centuries; others seem politically incorrect in the extreme, particularly when you consider that the rules were written by a woman. Do bear in mind that the Middle Ages were a violent time; jealousy taken to its violent conclusion was an accepted part of life, and women were as much to blame for this as men. If men loved to pull swords on each other to show how macho they were, women loved to taunt and tease them into doing so.

"closed" by returning it in a subsequent move. Each time a mill is closed another of the opponent's pieces is removed. In a "running mill," opening one mill will close another, so that a piece is removed every turn. If a player is unable to move any pieces because there are no empty points next to any pieces, then that player has lost the game. Otherwise, play continues until one player is reduced to three pieces.

The End Stage allows the player with only three pieces to move any one piece each turn to any empty point on the board, regardless of its position in relationship to his men. The other player must continue to move to adjacent empty points, unless both players are reduced to three pieces. The game ends when one player is down to two pieces and so can no longer form a mill.

PASS THE PARCEL

We don't know if this game is actually medieval in origin, but we have seen it played at a lot of living-history events, and it is great fun. It can also be played right at the feast table and makes a wonderful diversion between removes.

The "parcel" is made up of a series of cloth squares wrapped one inside the other, each tied securely with a piece of ribbon. Tucked inside each of the layers is either a prize or a forfeit. The parcel starts at one end of the table and is passed from guest to guest while musicians play. Whoever is holding the parcel when the musicians abruptly stop must unwrap one layer to find his or her prize or forfeit. Then the musicians begin again and the parcel continues on its way.

The prizes are no more than a foil-covered chocolate made to look like a coin (not exactly medieval,

1. The state of marriage does not properly excuse anyone from loving.
2. He who does not feel jealousy is not capable of loving.
3. No one can love two people at the same time.
4. It is well known that love is always either growing or declining.
5. Whatever a lover takes against his lover's will has no savor.
6. A male does not fall in love until he has reached full manhood.
7. A mourning period of two years for a deceased lover is required by the surviving partner.
8. No one should be prevented from loving except by reason of his own death.
9. No one can love unless compelled by the eloquence of love.
10. Love is an exile from the house of avarice.
11. It is unseemly to love anyone whom you would be ashamed to marry.
12. A true lover does not desire the passionate embraces of anyone but his beloved.
13. Love that is made public rarely lasts.
14. Love easily obtained is of little value; difficulty in obtaining it makes it precious.
15. Every lover regularly turns pale in the presence of his beloved.
16. On suddenly catching sight of his beloved, the heart of the lover begins to palpitate.
17. A new love drives out the old.
18. A good character alone makes someone worthy of love.
19. If love lessens, it soon fails and rarely recovers.
20. A man in love is always fearful.
21. The feeling of love is always increased by true jealousy.
22. When a lover feels suspicious of his beloved, jealousy, and with it, the sensation of love, are increased.
23. A man tormented by the thought of love eats and sleeps very little.
24. Everything a lover does ends in the thought of his beloved.
25. A true lover considers nothing good but what he thinks will please his beloved.
26. Love can deny nothing to love.
27. A lover cannot have too much of his lover's consolations.
28. A small supposition compels a lover to suspect his beloved of doing wrong.
29. A man who is troubled by excess lust does not usually love.
30. A true lover is continually and without interruption obsessed by the image of his beloved.
31. Nothing forbids one woman being loved by two men, or one man by two women.

A SIGN OF LOVE

For those of either sex who wish to express interest in someone at the feast, the proper medieval sign of intent is to offer a cloven fruit. Any piece of fruit is lightly studded with whole cloves. Custom dictates that the recipient of the cloven fruit pluck a clove from the fruit with his or her teeth and chew it up before offering a kiss in return. The origin of this curious custom can probably be explained by assuming that the clove would freshen the breath before the hoped-for kiss.

DICE

In the Middle Ages, dice came in a variety of interesting shapes, not just the square cubes we use. The spots, or pips, however, were arranged in the same way they are today. In addition to the games described here, dice are a good tool to use for choosing lots for contestants in many other games, such as blind man's buff, climbing the greased pole, and selecting the rotation in archery competitions.

Dice games in the Middle Ages, as now, seemed to invite gambling. There are recorded instances of men losing their sheep, their clothing, and even their wives and children in a game of dice. We do not recommend such heavy wagering as a way to make your medieval banquet a success.

1. The simplest dice game is for the players, numbering two or more, to add up their points toward a final score of one hundred. The order of play is decided by the players each taking a preliminary roll, the highest number rolling first, next highest number rolling second, and so on. The players throw the dice in turn, marking down their scores on a piece of paper. The first player to reach one hundred points or more wins. A little bit of tension can be brought to the game by demanding that the winning score be exactly one hundred. If a player has, let's say, ninety-six points, he must roll exactly four to win; any score above that does not count and the player loses a turn. If a player has a score of ninety-nine, he is eliminated

because it is impossible to roll a one when throwing a pair of dice.

2. Raffle requires three dice and is scored similarly to a game of poker. The object is to get all three dice to land with the same numbers showing or to throw pairs of the same number. If the highest throws involve two or more players with the same pairs, then the winner is determined by the number on the third die. For example, a pair of fives and a six will beat a pair of fives and a three.

3. Passage. The first player rolls three dice until he gets a pair of the same number. If the total of the pair is under ten, the player out, and loses. If it is over ten, he wins. If the throw is exactly ten, then the dice are passed to the next player but the cash pot or other wager is not collected.

HOODMAN'S BLIND
OR BLIND MAN'S BUFF

Unlike the Victorian version of this game, the medieval original had a lot more physical contact and was slightly rougher. One person is chosen by lot to be "it" and is blindfolded, either by having a bag pulled over the head or, in the truly medieval version, by having the hood of his lirapipe pulled down over the head. The player is then spun around several times and seeks to find his tormentors. Unlike later versions of the game, where the player simply wanders around in the dark while the rest of the players try to avoid him, in the medieval version the other players actively torment him by pulling at his clothes, shoving him, and striking at him with willow whips. In all-male versions of the game, the tormenting may have become fairly rough. It is this shoving, or buffeting, of the blind man that gives the game its name. When he successfully captures another player, he is released from darkness,

and the captured person becomes "it." There is no logical conclusion to the game.

CHILDREN'S GAMES

In addition to the above game, hoodman's blind, many other games were especially enjoyed by children. Surprisingly, most medieval children's games are still enjoyed by youngsters today. Hide and seek, seesaw, tag, and walking on stilts were all popular among medieval children.

Queek. Using a large, checkered cloth spread on a hard, smooth surface, or their parents' chessboard, children would throw pebbles on the board, calling out in advance whether the pebble would land on a light or dark square.

Stone Throwing. Then, as now, children could not resist throwing stones. Small stones were thrown for distance or at a target on the ground for accuracy.

OUTDOOR GAMES

Archery. Archery was one of the most common competition sports of the working man in medieval Europe and was particularly popular in England and Wales. Archers skilled with the Welsh longbow became the terror of the medieval battlefield. To ensure that their subjects were well practiced with the longbow, a succession of English kings outlawed all other forms of sport and decreed that every able-bodied man was to practice with the bow for at least two hours every Sunday.

To stage an archery competition, you need nothing more than a bale of straw, a simple bull's-eye target to attach to it, two good longbows, and a dozen or so arrows. The target should be painted white and inscribed with three concentric circles, the largest of them about thirty inches in diameter. The smallest circle, at the center of the target, should be about five inches in diameter and colored red.

Depending on their level of skill, contestants should stand anywhere from fifty to two hundred yards from the target. It requires a fairly skilled archer to hit the target, let alone the bull's-eye, at two hundred yards, but the Welsh longbow has an effective range of up to four hundred yards.

Contestants loose, or shoot, in rotation, one arrow per round. In traditional medieval archery competitions, a total of three rounds were taken. The contestant coming closest to the bull's-eye was declared the winner of the match. A complete archery contest consists of a series of elimination matches, with

The tilt was immensely popular among the nobility, who used it as a display of and training ground for mounted warfare. It could also be lucrative for the contestants. On winning a tilt, a knight had the right to claim the armor, and sometimes the horse, of his defeated opponent.

While we do not suggest holding an actual joust, we have come up with an alternative that can be challenging, enjoyable, and holds a good degree of excitement. The "knights" face each other on a "jousting horse," a log or pole eighteen to twenty feet in length and eight to ten inches in diameter. A discarded telephone pole will serve the purpose, but to avoid the possibility of injury, it must be free from all nails and splinters. The length provides the combatants room to move, and the diameter is necessary to support their combined weight.

This pole should be supported on two tripods, four feet in length, set about eighteen inches from each end of the pole. The tripods should be made from nothing less than four-by-four posts, to ensure good support. Two legs of the tripod should cross in such a way that they form a saddle for the pole to set in. The third leg simply ensures that the structure dose not collapse from the movement of the jousters. The structure should be bolted together, as shown in the construction diagram, with quarter-inch-diameter lag bolts. The tripods must be staked firmly into the ground to ensure that they do not collapse under the jostling that will take place on the pole. See the accompanying illustration for full construction details. We recommend that you enlist the help of someone familiar with construction techniques when building the structure.

To hold the tournament, two challengers straddle the pole, one at each end. Each "knight" is armed with a bag of tightly packed straw the size of a pillowcase. The men shinny toward each other on the pole. When they get within reach, they swing at each other with the bags of straw in an attempt to "unhorse" their opponent. Swinging too fast or too early can unbalance a knight, giving the opponent an early advantage. You will be surprised just how exciting this can get. Whether the winner is awarded a prize or the loser is required to surrender his armor and horse to his opponent is up to you.

The Palio Race. In medieval Italy, the sporting event of the year was undoubtedly the palio race. The

A modernized version of the medieval Italian palio horse race has contestants riding piggy-back in a mad scramble toward the finish line.

palio was a wild, free-for-all horse race through the streets of the city, each horse being backed by a local company, merchants' guild, or neighborhood. Beginning in 1275, several Italian city-states held palio races, the most prominent being Siena, which still holds the race every year. The object was to back the horse that crossed the finish line first. Being medieval Italy, there were no set rules. Unhorsing an opponent, or even killing him, was all part of the game. The winning horse did not have to have its rider when it crossed the finish line, and even if the rider was there, he did not have to be alive. There was no second place. The palio itself was a bolt of expensive cloth that was presented to the owner or sponsor of the winning horse.

While we do not expect you to stage an actual horse race, nor do we recommend killing any of your contestants, we have devised an amusing alternative to this breathtaking event. The course of our version of the race may be either a straight line (usually no more than one hundred yards) or a circle around a building. If you have space to plot out a more interesting course, all the better, but it is not necessary. Any number of two-person teams may enter the race. One member of the team will serve as the rider, the other as the horse. Riders (preferably small women or teenagers) mount their trusty steeds (men eager to display their athletic prowess) by sitting on their shoulders and locking their legs under the men's armpits.

Gather your teams at the starting line, and tell the riders to mount up. When everyone is mounted (this alone can be a source of great fun for the spectators), they should line up evenly along the starting line. At a predetermined signal, the race begins. There are no other rules. Pushing, shoving, and spitting mouthfuls of water at opponents is encouraged, and the rider need not be on the winning horse when it crosses the finish line. Cheers, jeers, and shouts of encouragement from the sidelines are encouraged to keep up the tension and competitive spirit. Presentation of five or six yards of fine fabric to the winning rider is both historically correct and a real crowd pleaser, and a box of oatmeal presented to the winning horse is the perfect ending to this absurd bit of horseplay.

Wrestling. Wrestling was universally popular among male members of the working and peasant classes during the Middle Ages. No equipment was necessary, and the rules seem to have been pretty much made up on the spot. Combatants could either fight to a throw, until one of them successfully pinned the other to the ground (at the shoulders, hips, or any

combination thereof), or until one of the men upset the balance of the other and forced him outside the boundary of a "ring," a circle four to six feet in diameter that had been drawn in the dust.

One unusual variation on wrestling took place when the contestants sat on the shoulders of two other men and carried out their competition in the air. The object here was to send one's opponent tumbling to the ground.

Tug of War. This familiar game is perfectly medieval and still a lot of fun today. All that is required are two teams and a length of stout rope. We recommend using a one-inch-diameter hemp rope if possible. The diameter gives the contestants something to grip, and hemp is less likely to stretch than plastic or nylon. No matter what kind of rope is being used, we recommend that contestants wear gloves, as our hands are just not as tough and calloused as those of medieval farmers and soldiers.

To make the game more authentically medieval, the teams should assemble on either side of a hazard. This could be a low wall, a hedge, a mud puddle, or a stream. On a signal, each team tries to pull the other off balance and across or into the hazard. The game ends when one side encounters the hazard or gives up in sheer exhaustion.

Stone Throwing. This game is not very sophisticated sounding but is a good test of skill and strength, depending on the size of the stones being thrown. Small stones that could be held in the palm of the hand were generally thrown for distance and accuracy, frequently at some predetermined target. Larger stones, sometimes weighing up to fifty or sixty pounds, were thrown for distance. Remnants of this last still exist in Scottish and Swiss games and were the precursor to the Olympic sport of shot putting.

Climbing a Greased Pole. The object of this game is for contestants to climb to the top of a greased pole and claim a prize. The prize, traditionally a haunch of meat, was sometimes tethered to the top of the pole and had to be pulled loose, or its place was taken by a ribbon, which also had to be pulled from the pole. In some instances, the winner was simply the first person to climb high enough to lay the flat of his hand on top of the pole.

The pole should be eight to twelve inches in diameter and fifteen to sixteen feet in length. The diameter allows the contestants to gain some kind of hold on the pole, no matter how slight, and the length allows for five feet of the pole to be buried firmly in the ground and still leave ten or more feet exposed for climbing. The pole must be completely smooth. Any splinters can cause injuries, and rough spots or knots can give a climber an unfair advantage. The portion of the pole to be buried in the ground must be firmly enough anchored that the pole will not tilt to one side as it is repeatedly assaulted by contestants attempting to reach the top. When the pole is firmly fixed in the ground, it should be covered with a solid lubricant that will not run off, such as lard or shortening.

Contestants determine the order of play by drawing lots. The first contestant who successfully reaches the top of the pole or pulls down the prize wins. The biggest problem is the mess that the competition makes of contestants' clothes. Considering the lack of practice most of us have in climbing poles these days, the game will probably work just as well if the pole is not greased.

Catching a Greased Pig. In the modern world, few of us have access to a piglet. If you do, pick one that is small enough to be caught but big enough to run away from its pursuers—two to three months of age should do nicely. The game will need to take place in a well-fenced area so neither the pig nor the contestants can escape.

Greasing the animal with lard or shortening will ensure a good, slippery pig. Traditionally, the contestants surrounded the fenced area. The referee entered the ring, carrying the pig in a feed bag. When he reached the center of the ring, the pig was released and the insanity began. The person who successfully captured the little fellow got to take him home and either raise him or have him for dinner.

Practically speaking, there are few of us who have access to, or use for, a two-month-old pig. Fewer still would have the heart to kill and eat it. A fairly reasonable facsimile can be played, however, by greasing a soccer ball or basketball. It may not run and squeal, but its round shape makes it very hard to keep hold of when six or eight people are all fighting for possession at the same time.

A summertime variant of this game takes place in the water, where a greased watermelon may be substituted for the pig. Swimmers must catch hold of the

"pig" and move it safely to one of two designated spots. This is not as easy as it may sound, especially as everyone is trying for the same "pig."

Blood Sports. The hardships and brutal realities of the medieval world placed a fairly low value on human life. It is not surprising, then, that an even lower value was placed on the lives of animals. We include a brief description of these "sports" only as an insight into the medieval mind, certainly not as a recommendation that any of these horrible activities be recreated in any form.

In bull and bear baiting, a captured bear or a bull was tethered to a pole in the center of a large pit. A pack of specially trained hunting dogs was then turned loose on the restrained animal. As with most such games, betting on the outcome was an integral part of the play. A winner was declared when either the bull or the bear had killed all of the dogs, or the dogs had torn the frenzied animal to pieces.

In dog and cock fights, a pair of dogs or roosters that had been trained to attack their own kind would be released into a ring, or pit, and tear at each other until one of them was dead. Amazing as it seems today, cock fighting was considered a perfectly acceptable sport for boys over ten or twelve years of age. Similarly, cock throwing involved boys chasing down a rooster while pelting it with stones. A good, stunning blow disabled the bird, thereby allowing its capture. Even worse, in Italy and France, teenage boys would impress their girlfriends by nailing a live cat to a tree and proceeding to batter the tortured animal to death with their heads.

CHAPTER 12

ROBYN HODE: A MUMMERS PLAY

This and numerous other mummers plays have been performed since early medieval times. The lines were frequently not written down until the eighteenth or nineteenth century, so there is little original text available, but since there were unlimited variations to the stories, there were never any "correct" versions. This version of the play is probably nineteenth-century in origin. As in most mummers plays, there are no written stage directions to accompany the script. The actors simply pantomimed the action dictated by the lines they were speaking, or often the lines were narrated off stage. It is always best if the actors rehearse the play ahead of time and learn their lines by heart, but in medieval times, members of the audience sometimes volunteered to serve as impromptu members of the cast, reading their lines when their turns came (assuming they could read). It is perfectly acceptable, even expected, for the audience to cheer the hero, hiss and boo the villain, and applaud and laugh as appropriate. One entertaining variation to the standard play is for the actors to be selected from the audience, while the play is narrated from the side of the stage. The actors then need to improvise along with the story.

This particular play was intended for use at Christmas, but if you want to use the play at some other time, we suggest simply substituting the lines below for the first five lines. The revised lines also refer to some of the dishes on the suggested menu:

> The end of our feast is drawing near,
> We hope it brought you all good cheer.
> Roast pork, cherry potage, and game pie,
> Who likes these things better than I?
> Medieval fare makes us dance and sing . . .

CAST

Friar Tuck: a fat monk

Green Man: the spirit of the woods, probably an ancient pagan spirit

Sir Guy of Guisbourne: a nobleman, the villain of the play

Robyn Hode: the hero

Saracen: a Turkish alchemist with magical powers

Musicians and Dancing Bear: (optional) characters who signal the joyous conclusion of the play

THE PLAY

FRIAR TUCK: Christmas comes but once a year,
    And when it comes, it brings good cheer.
    Roast beef, plum pudding, and mince pie,
    Who likes these things better than I?
    Christmas fare makes us dance and sing,
    Money in the purse is a capital thing.
    Gentles all give what you please,
    The green man comes to welcomely receive.

GREEN MAN: In come I, the jolly green man, welcome or
    welcome not.
    I hope the old green man will not be forgot.
    Although we've come, we've but a short time to stay,
    But we'll bring you sport and pastime before we go away.
    Room, room, gentles I pray,
    For I now bring Sir Guy of Guisbourne this way.

SIR GUY: In come I, Guy of Guisbourne, lately come from
    France,
    And with the Sheriff of Nottingham's men
    I'll make that wolf's head dance.
    And if Robyn Hode were here, I wonder what would
    appear?
    I'd cut him up as small as mint dust [draws sword]
    And send him to old Friar Tuck to make a pie crust.

ROBYN HODE: In come I, Robyn Hode, from Sherwood did
    I spring,
    And with my bow and merry men, I'll make that
    Guisbourne sting.
    I'll take from the rich and give to the poor
    And guard Old England for Richard our King.
    I'll fight Guisbourne with courage bold;
    If his blood's hot, I'll make it cold.

SIR GUY: Down under thee I'll never bow nor bend;
    I never took thee to be my friend.

ROBYN: For why, for why, sir, did I ever do you any harm?

SIR GUY: You saucy man, you ought to be stabbed!

ROBYN: Stab for stab, that is my fear.
    Appoint me the place, and I'll meet you there.

SIR GUY: My place is pointing on the ground,
    Where I mean to lay your body down!

ROBYN: Pull out your sword and fight!
    Pull out your purse and pay!
    For once, satisfaction I will have
    Before I go away.

SIR GUY: No money will I pull out nor pay,
    But you and I must fight this battle most manfully.
    Bold and slasher is my name;
    With sword in hand, I aim to win this game.
    My head is made of iron, my body lined with steel,

And brass unto my knuckle bones, I'll fight you in this
    field.

ROBYN: Stand off, stand off, Sir Guy, or by my sword soon
    you'll die.
    I'll cut doublet through and through
    And make thy buttons fly.
    I've traveled o'er England, France, and Spain
    And many a dog I have slain.
    For what our king shall have is right,
    This nasty man I'll now fight.

[Robyn and Sir Guy fight, while the crowd shouts encouragement. Sir Guy slays Robyn.]

SIR GUY: Behold, behold, what I have done.
    I cut him down like the evening sun.
    And ten more of such men I'll fight,
    For what the sheriff shall have is right.

FRIAR TUCK: Alas, alas, poor Robyn's slain,
    Between two arms his body's lain.
    For what some doctor must come and see
    Where this man lies bleeding at his feet.
    Oh, is there a doctor to be found
    To raise this poor man from the ground?
    I would pay a full five pounds
    If there were a doctor to be found.

[Enter a Saracen.]

SARACEN: In come I, Ahmed the Good,
    With my hand I can stop the blood.
    I can stop the blood and heal thy wound
    and raise this man from the ground.

FRIAR TUCK: What can you cure?

SARACEN: I can cure the hipsy, pipsy, palsey, or gout,
    Strain within or strain without.
    If a man's neck be broke, I'll set it again,
    or else I won't have a penny for my fee.

FRIAR TUCK: What's your fee?

SARACEN: Ten pounds.

FRIAR TUCK: Ten pounds!
    I can't pay as much as that.

SARACEN: Saddle my horse and I'll be gone.

FRIAR TUCK: Stop, stop, oh wondrous one.
    What is your lowest fee?

SARACEN: Nine pounds, nineteen shillings, and eleven
    pence,
    And that's a penny under price, because you're a poor
    friar.

FRIAR TUCK: Better try thy skill.

SARACEN: I have here a potion, brought from the east.
    It is called the golden elixir, and with one drop,
    I will revive Robyn Hode with these magic words:
    "Sim Salabim."
    Rise up young man
    And see how your body can walk and sing.

ROBYN: I now waken from my sleep, but friends, I cannot
    stay.

I must continue on the fight
To curb the sheriff's evil ways.
Before I go, however, a boon I ask, I pray.
Dig deep in your purses for the doctor's bill to pay.

[Enter musicians and dancing bear.]

[This is a perfect time to collect for a local charity.]

CHAPTER 13

SONGS, BALLADS, AND CAROLS

◆

M usic has always been, and continues to be, an integral part of festivities, both public and private. During the Middle Ages, however, it was largely up to the participants to make the music themselves. With luck, the host was wealthy enough to keep court musicians, or at least hire a few minstrels to provide background music and lead the company in favorite songs, as well as introduce them to new ones. Certainly, many of the songs in this chapter will be new to you and your guests, but you may be surprised at how many of them you already know, especially the Christmas carols.

The main problem you will face will be providing background music to accompany the singing and also to play throughout much of the feast. A partial solution can be provided by the wide selection of medieval music available on cassette and CD. This will at least keep the natives from becoming restless during the meal, and at best establish an ideal atmosphere for your feast. When the time comes to raise voices in song, there are several possible options. If you live near a college or university, there may be a medieval recreationist group that counts among its number a few musicians who might be enticed or hired to play for a few hours. You would be amazed at how eager these individuals are to share their talents with members of the public.

Alternatively, the college music department likely has a few students or faculty members familiar with medieval music, and they may even have medieval-type instruments that will provide a realistic sound for your event. While these professional or semi-professional musicians may not come as inexpensively as medieval reenactors, the possibility of proper period instruments will make it well worth the difference.

If you or your event is associated with a church, you might entice at least part of the choir to lead the audience in song. Lacking other instruments, a piano or portable organ may have to suffice for musical accompaniment.

If your medieval guest list is going to number into the hundreds, it might be wise to arrange much of the music to be performed concert style, with the guests invited to join in on a few selected numbers. Whatever the case, have the songs photocopied and available to guests. It is probably best to pass out the song sheets just prior to the time they will be used; otherwise, they will tend to get lost over the course of the day.

Before you launch yourself into song, it is good to understand just how medieval songs differed from their modern counterparts. Following are some brief notes on a number of medieval song types.

BALLADS
Ballads (see pages 85–94) were the pop music of the medieval world. Usually in the form of a narrative

story, ballads told about love, adventure, bravery, and great sadness—the same things that are still prime elements in poetry and music. The difference between music in the Middle Ages and today's music is that seven hundred years ago, ballads were also a primary source of news. When a great battle had been fought, a king had died, or a rich lord had married off his idiot heir, the event was immediately put into a song that served as both entertainment and a source of news. This timely music was then carried from place to place by minstrels or troubadors who studied long and hard to be able to remember the complete text of the ballads, which sometimes ran to five or six thousand words. A good memory was essential in a world where literacy was a rarity, and the hunger for entertaining stories and news of any kind was voracious.

CHRISTMAS CAROLS

The singing of songs in celebration of Christmas dates from the very early Middle Ages. But unlike today, when wandering carolers are one of the more charming and old-fashioned aspects of the season, the public singing of carols was once outlawed by both church and secular authorities. Since bands of carolers usually collected money from passersby, they were considered beggars, and therefore an undesirable social element. The prohibitions against carol singing obviously failed. Thanks to the failure of this legislation, we can still enjoy these wonderful songs. The carols presented here (see pages 94–103) include some familiar selections and some that will probably be unfamiliar. We hope some of these will find their way to becoming a part of your personal list of favorite Christmas carols. All these songs date from the fourteenth and fifteenth centuries.

One of the most popular secular Christmas songs today is "The Twelve Days of Christmas." But the familiar refrains of "five golden rings, four calling birds, three French hens, two turtledoves, and a partridge in a pear tree" were only standardized in the nineteenth century. Originally this was a free-form song, in which the first singer would invent his own "gift." When

another singer took up the second verse, he would add his own "gift" and repeat the first singer's verse. The verses might just as easily have been "five barking dogs, four casks of ale, three thrusting daggers, two velvet gowns, and a necklace of tiny white pearls." The song was more a memory game to entertain dinner guests than a familiar song to be sung by rote. Try doing it this way; it may be a real challenge, but the results are likely to be amusing. Because the song involves the Twelve Days of Christmas, it is especially appropriate on Twelfth Night (January 5), the traditional end of the Christmas season.

EASTER CAROLS

Although they have now disappeared entirely, Easter carols were once as common as Christmas carols. We hope you will find this Easter carol (see pages 104–105) as delightful and interesting as we do.

MOTHER'S DAY CAROLS

Most of us think of Mother's Day as a fairly modern invention; in the United States, it was only institutionalized during Franklin Roosevelt's administration. In fact, Mother's Day (or Mothering Sunday, as it is called in Great Britain) dates to the late fourteenth or early fifteenth century. The celebration of motherhood was always celebrated during the Lenten season. The rare Mothering Sunday carol included here (see pages 106–108) dates from about 1450.

FURRY DAY CAROLS

During the Middle Ages, "furry days" were those rare days that were not specifically associated with any particular religious observance. The word *furry* is an English corruption of the old French word *feire*, which translated to the English word *faire*, or *fair* in modern English. It was on these furry days that village fetes or fairs were traditionally scheduled, so that they did not interfere with more sacred festivities. Furry carols, like the summer carol, can be sung during any of the warmer months of the year (see pages 109–110).

DOWN IN YON FOREST

Solo Down in yon for-est there stands a hall: *Chorus* The
Ring, ... The

Soli

Ring, ... The

bells of Par-a-dise I heard them ring : *Solo* It's cov-er'd all o-ver with
bells of Par-a-dise I heard them ring : Ring, ...

Soli

bells .... I heard them ring : Ring, ...

Chorus pur-ple and pall : And I love my Lord Je-sus a-bove a-ny-thing.
.... And I love my Lord Je-sus a-bove a-ny-thing.

.... And I love Je-sus a-bove a-ny-thing.

2. In that hall there stands a bed:
   It's covered all over with scarlet so red:

3. At the bedside there lies a stone:
   Which the sweet Virgin Mary knelt upon:

4. Under that bed there runs a flood:
   The one half runs water, the other runs blood:

5. At the bed's foot there grows a thorn:
   Which ever blows blossom since he was born:

6. Over that bed the moon shines bright:
   denoting our Saviour was born this night:

THE HUNT IS UP!

Old English
Arr. by GEOFFREY SHAW

The hunt is up, . . the hunt is up, . . And it is well nigh day, ... And Har-ry, our King, is gone hunt-ing . . . To bring his deer . . to bay . . . .

2. The East is bright with morning light,
   And darkness it is fled;
   The merry horn wakes up the morn
   To leave his idle bed.

3. The sun is glad to see us clad
   All in our lusty green,
   And smiles in the sky, as he riseth high
   To see and to be seen.

4. Awake, all men, I say again,
   Be merry as you may,
   For Harry, our King, is gone hunting
   To bring his deer to bay.

BARLEY MOW

from collection of National English Airs
pub. Chappell Publishers, London 1840

Moderately fast and in a Jovial style

Bass by Warren

And we'll drink out of the nipperkin boys, good health to the Bar - ley Mow . . . . . . And

we'll drink out of the pipperkin boys, good health to the Bar - ley Mow . . . . . . The nipperkin pipperkin

Slower

Chorus in the first time

and the brown bowl, good health to the Bar - ley mow my boys, good health to the Bar - ley Mow . . . .

2. And we'll drink out of the well boys,
   Good health to the barley-mow.
   And we'll drink out of the well boys,
   Good health to the barley-mow.
          The nipperkin, pipperkin, etc.

3. And we'll drink out of the lake boys,
   Good health to the barley-mow.
   And we'll drink out of the lake boys,
   Good health to the barley-mow.
          The nipperkin, pipperkin, etc.

BRING US GOOD ALE

Bring us in good ale, good ale, And bring us in good
ale For our bless-ed La-dy's sake, Bring us in good ale.

Bring us in no brown bread, for that is made of bran, Nor
bring us in no white bread, for there in is no gain. But
bring us in good ale, good ale, And bring us in good ale, For
our bless-ed La-dy's sake, bring us in good ale.

2. Bring us in no beef, for there is many bones,
   But bring us in good ale, for that go'th down at once:

3. Bring us in no bacon, for that is passing fat,
   But bring us in good ale, and give us enough of that:

4. Bring us in no mutton, for that is passing lean,
   Nor bring us in no tripes, for they be seldom clean:

5. Bring us in no eggs, for there are many shells,
   But bring us in good ale, and give us nothing else:

6. Bring us in no butter, for therein are many hairs,
   Nor bring us in no pig's flesh, for that will make us bears:

7. Bring us in no puddings, for therein is all God's good,
   Nor bring us in no venison, that is not for our blood:

8. Bring us in no capon's flesh, for that is often dear,
   Nor bring us in no duck's flesh, for the slobber in the mere (mire):

SUMMER IS A COMING IN

THE AIR FROM A MANUSCRIPT SIX HUNDRED YEARS OLD.

Words modernized

Sum-mer is a coming in, Loudly sing, Cuck-oo! Meadows green a-round are seen Be-

-spangled o'er with dew, Sing, Cuck-oo! Young Alein, the shepherd swain, Is gath'ring vio-lets

blue; He will car-ry wreaths to Ma-ry, Glad as thou, Cuckoo, Cuck-oo, Cuck-oo, We

welcome thee, Cuck-oo, That wak'st the world a-new.

Prophet of the merry throat, Loudly sing, Cuckoo! For thou bring'st, whene'er thou sing'st, Good

tidings, aye and true: Sing, Cuck-oo! Mary's love may fickle prove, False hopes the swain may

rue: May's returning, falsehood spurning, Singest thou, Cuckoo! Cuckoo! Cuck-oo! Hail,

bird of truth! Cuck-oo! That wak'st the world a-new.

SOMERSET WASSAIL

(CHRISTMAS AND NEW YEAR, SECULAR)
Traditional
Oxford University Press, 1923

In Quick Time. Voices in Unison (Semi-Chorus)

(M. S.)

Was - sail, and was - sail, all o - o-ver the town the
cu - p it is white and the a - ale it is brown the cu - up it is
made of the go - od ash - en tree A - nd so - o is the malt of the

Chorus

best b - ar - ley for it's your was - ail, and it's our was -

-sail and it's joy be to you and a jol-ly was-sail

2. O master and missus, are you all within?
   Pray open the door and let us come in;
   O master and missus a-sitting by the fire,
   Pray think upon poor travellers, a-travelling
        in the mire:

Chorus

3. O where is the maid, with the silver-headed pin,
   To open the door, and let us come in?
   O master and missus, it is our desire
   A good loaf and cheese, and a toast by the fire:

Chorus

4. There was an old man, and he had an old cow,
   And how for to keep her he didn't know how,
   He built up a barn for to keep his cow warm,
   And a drop or two of cider will do us no harm:

   No harm, boys, harm; no harm, boys, harm;
   And a drop or two of cider will do us no harm.

5. The girt dog of Langport he burnt his long tail,
   And this is the night we go singing wassail:
   O master and missus, now we must be gone:
   God bless all in this house till we do come again.

   For it's your wassail, and it's our wassail!
   And it's joy be to you, and a jolly wassail!

IN EXCELSIS GLORIA

(NATIVITY)
First Tune
A. H. Brown

When Christ was born of Ma - ry free, In Beth - lem in that fair ci - ty,

Angels sung e'er with mirth and glee, In ex - cel - sis glo - ri - a,

In ex-cel-si glo-ri-a, In ex-cel-sis glo-ri-a,

In ex-cel-sis glo-ri-a, In ex-cel-sis glo-ri-a.

D.S.

Verse 2

Herd-men be-held, &c.

Verse 4

Then, dear Lord, &c.

Christo paremus cantica,
In excelsis gloria.

2. Herdmen beheld these angels bright—
   To them appeared with great light.
   And said, 'God's son is born this night':

3. This king is come to save his kind,
   In the scripture as we find;
   Therefore this song have we in mind:

4. Then, dear Lord, for thy great grace,
   Grant us the bliss to see thy face,
   Where we may sing to thy solace:

NOWELL, NOWELL: IN BETHLEM

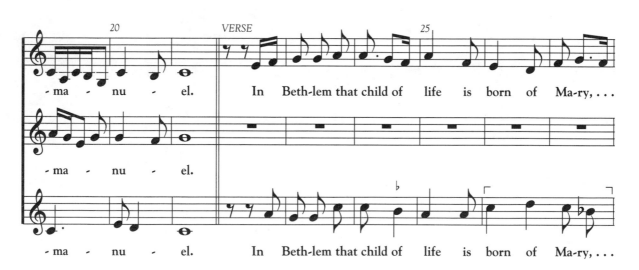

mai-den and wife; he is both God and.... man,... take shrift; no - well.

mai-den and wife; he is both God and man,... take shrift; no - well.

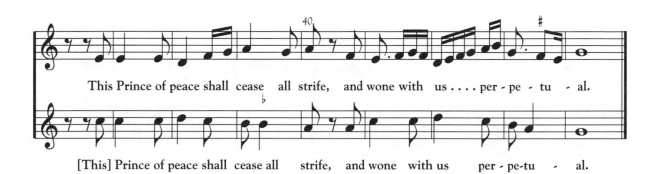

This Prince of peace shall cease all strife, and wone with us.... per-pe-tu - al.

[This] Prince of peace shall cease all strife, and wone with us per-pe-tu - al.

2. This child shall buy us with his blood
   And be nailëd on a rood;
   His ransom passeth all earthly good,
   Nowell!
   Alas what wight dare be so wood
   To slay so gentle a jewel?

3. By his powst this child shall rise;
   Fro hell he shall take his emprise
   And save mankind in this wise;
   Nowell!
   Thus telleth us the prophecies,
   Herebeforn as they did tell.

MAKE US MERRY

R, ff.12v.-13

VERSE 25 30

Ga - bri - el, . . . brighter . . . . . . than . . . . the . . . . sun, gra - cious-ly . . . . greet - ë . . .

Ga - bri - el, . . . brighter . . . . . than . . . . the . . . . . . sun, gra - cious - ly . . greet - ë . . .

35

that . . . . mai - den . . free; tho - rough her meekness Christ . . . . have we . . . found;

that . . . . mai - den . . free; tho - rough her meek - ness Christ . . have we . . . . . . found;

40 45

Ec - ce, an - cilla Domi - ni . . . .

Ec - ce, an - cil - la Do - mi - ni . . . .

2. Ave Maria, virgin bright;
   We joyeth of the benignity;
   The Holy Ghost is in thee light;
   Thou hast conceivëd thy Son so free.

3. Now is that maidë great with child,
   Herself alone also credibly;
   Fro the fiend she shall us shield,
   so sayeth bookës in their story.

101

YEOMAN'S CAROL

(CHRISTMAS)

Church-gallery book

(M. S.)

Let Christ - ians all with joy - ful mirth, Both young and

old, both great and small, now think up - on our

sav - ior's birth who brought sal - va - tion to us all.

Chorus

This day did Christ man's soul from dea - th re - move,

with glor - ious saints to dwell in Heaven a - bove.

2. No palace, but an ox's stall,
   The place of his nativity;
   This truly should instruct us all
   To learn of him humility:

Chorus

3. Then Joseph and the Virgin came
   Unto the town of Bethlehem,
   But sought in vain within the same
   For lodging to be granted them:

Chorus

4. A stable harboured them, where they
   Continued till this blessed morn.
   Let us rcjoice and keep the day,
   Wherein the Lord of life was born:

Chorus

5. He that descended from above,
   Who for your sins has meekly died,
   Make him the pattern of your love;
   So will your joys be sanctified:

Chorus

EASTER CAROL

French tune
N. S. T.
Oxford University Press, 1923

(M. S.)

Cheer up, friends and neigh - bours, now it's East - er tide

Stop from end - less la - bours wor - ries put a - side

Men should rise from sad - ness e - vil fol - ly strife

When God's mi - ghty glad - ness brings the earth to life.

2. Out from snowdrifts chilly,
   Roused from drowsy hours,
   Bluebell wakes, and lily;
   God calls up the flowers!
   Into life he raises
   All the sleeping buds;
   Meadows weave his praises,
   And the spangled woods.

3. All his truth and beauty,
   All his righteousness,
   Are our joy and duty,
   Bearing his impress:
   Look! the earth waits breathless
   After Winter's strift:
   Easter shows man deathless,
   Spring leads death to life.

4. Ours the more and less is;
   But, changeless all the days,
   God revives and blesses,
   Like the sunlight rays.
   'All mankind is risen,'
   The Easter bells do ring,
   While from out their prison
   Creep the flowers of Spring!

MOTHERING SUNDAY

(MID-LENT)

'He who goes a-mothering finds violets in the lane.'

German, 14th century
George Hare Leonard

Sopranos sing words, other parts hum accompaniment

(M. S.)

It is the day of all the year, of all the year the one day

When I shall see my mo-ther dear and bring her cheer a-mothering on Sun-day

Faux Bourdon Version for choice of verses
Tenors sign words, other parts hum accompaniment

For Last Verse all sing words

It is the day of all the year, of all the year the one day

and here come I my mother dear to bring you cheer a-mo-the-ring on Sun-day

2. So I'll put on my Sunday coat,
   And in my hat a feather,
   And get the lines I writ by rote,
   With many a note,
   That I've a-strung together.

3. And now to fetch my wheaten cake,
   To fetch it from the baker,
   He promised me, for Mother's sake,
   The best he'd bake
   For me to fetch and take her.

4. Well have I known, as I went
       by
   One hollow lane, that none day
   I'd fail to find—for all they're
       shy—
   Where violets lie,
   As I went home on Sunday.

5. My sister Jane is waiting-maid
   Along with Squire's lady;
   And year by year her part she's
   And home she stayed,   [played,
   To get the dinner ready.

6. For Mother'll come to Church
       you'll see—
   Of all the year it's the day—
   'The one,' she'll say, 'that's made
   And so it be: [for me.'
   It's every Mother's free day.

7. The boys will all come home from
       town,
   Not one will miss that one day;
   And every maid will bustle down
   To show her gown,
   A-Mothering on Sunday.

8. It is the day of all the year,
   Of all the year the one day;
   And here come I, my Mother dear,
   To bring you cheer,
   A-Mothering on Sunday.

FURRY DAY CAROL

(MAY)
Traditional
Oxford University Press, 1923

(M. S.)

Re - e - mem - ber us poor Ma - yers all And thus we do

Be - gin - a to lead our lives in right - eous - ness

or else we die in - sin - a With Ho - lan - to

Ho - lan - to,   Ho - lan - to, sing   mer - - ry,

2. We have been rambling half the night,
   And almost all the day-a,
   And now, returnèd back again,
   We've brought you a branch of many-a:

Chorus

3. O, we were up as soon as day,
   To fetch the summer home-a;
   The summer is a coming-on,
   And winter is agone-a:

Chorus

4. Then let us all most merry be,
   And sing with cheerful voice-a;
   For we have good occasion now
   This time for to rejoice-a:

Chorus

5. Saint George he next shall be our song:
   Saint George, he was a knight-a;
   Of all the men in Christendom
   Saint George he was the right-a:

Chorus

6. God bless our land with power and might,
   God send us peace in England;
   Pray send us peace in England;
   For ever in merry England:

Chorus

CHAPTER 14
DANCES

◆

Dance has always been a part of human celebration, whether religious or secular. Ever since people first learned to drum a simple beat on a hollow log, they have been tapping their toes and moving their feet in time with the rhythm. This chapter will provide all you need to know to learn and teach simple medieval dance. If you would like to introduce the dance at your medieval event, there are a few considerations. If your event is relatively small, under one hundred people, it should be no problem for one or two couples to learn the steps and teach them to any interested guests. If, on the other hand, you are expecting several hundred people, it might be wiser to find four or five couples who would be willing to learn the dances and perform them during or after the feast as a form of entertainment. Trying to teach two hundred people how to dance, particularly if they have had a few drinks, might be more confusion than you will want to deal with.

Unfortunately, there are virtually no documented dance steps surviving from earlier than 1400. There is earlier surviving dance music, but we do not know which steps were danced to it, and we are not even sure of the speed at which the music should be played, so we will concentrate on dances of the fifteenth century. Fifteenth-century dance fell into two basic styles: the Burgundian style and the Italian style. Burgundian refers to those dances generally found in high-court

circles. They were very fancy, with lots of elegant patterns and athletic leaping in the air. The people who practiced these dances considered dance an essential part of a courtly education; they spent a lot of time at it and often got quite good. The Italian style was far simpler. These were the dances of the middle classes, used on those occasions when hard-working merchants held or attended a feast, wedding, or other celebration. Though it is called Italian, it was common in England and was probably the basic style of dance found in most western European countries. The three dances in this chapter are well-documented fifteenth-century French dances in the Italian style.

Our dances come from a book entitled *Orchésographie*. Written by a French ecclesiastic named Jean Tabourot, *Orchésographie* was first published in 1588 and supplies a wealth of detail on dancing. Unlike many other period sources, it supplies details of steps, dances, and music, along with timings, drum rhythms, and useful social nuances ("spit and blow your nose sparingly"). Tabourot says that some of the dances in his book are old ("Our predecessors danced pavans, basse dances, branles and corantos . . ."), and we know that the dances below date to at least the 1400s. In all, the book describes the Basse dance, the Pavan, Pavane d'Espagne, Courante, Allemande, Volte, Canary, Morisque, a sword dance called Les Bouffons, fifteen Galliard variations, and twenty-five Branles. The entire book is written in the form of a dialogue between a dancing master called Arbeau and his student Capriol. To give you a feel for the original book, we have retained bits of the conversation between the two characters throughout the instructions.

> Capriol: "I much enjoyed fencing and tennis and this placed me on friendly terms with young men. However, without a knowledge of dancing, I could not please the damsels, upon whom, it seems to me, the entire reputation of an eligible young man depends."

> Arbeau: "Kings and princes are wont to command performances of dancing and masquerades to salute, entertain and give joyous greetings to foreign nobles. We take part in such rejoicing to celebrate wedding days and in the rites of our religious festivals."

There are some general observations that can be applied to all medieval dances, and it is good to keep them in mind when you are learning the steps. During the Middle Ages, most dances, whether they were executed in the court of a great king or stomped out on the village green by a bunch of plowmen and their wives, would look to us like folk dances. They were danced in a line, two or more lines, a circle, or a series of circles. It is only the complexity of the steps that separated upper-class dance from peasant dance. If you don't get them the first time around, don't feel bad. As Arbeau says to his student, "Every dancer acquits himself to the best of his ability, each according to his years and degree of skill."

Assuming that most people at your medieval event will not know these dances, it might be best if you have one couple, or at least one individual, who can act as dance master, leading everyone through the individual steps, and at least one dance, before the actual dancing begins.

THE BASIC STEPS

When you have committed these seven basic steps to memory, you will be able to perform all three dances below, hopefully like a pro, in no time.

Révérence

To perform the révérence, you will keep the left foot firmly upon the ground and bending the right knee take the point of the toe behind the left foot, removing your bonnet or hat the while and bowing to your damsel and the company.

The révérence was the opening movement of most dances; it was no more than a way to pay honor to the lady with whom a man was dancing. Reverencing in the correct fashion was considered very important; some dancing manuals devoted whole chapters to it.

Pieds Joints

Pieds joints . . . is considered to be the correct position when the feet are placed side by side, the toes in a straight line and the dancer's weight equally distributed on both feet.

Pieds joints is no more than standing up straight with your feet together. If you can't figure this one out, you may want to consider leaving the dance floor.

Simples

You will perform a simple by making a pied largi with the right foot and to conclude a pied joint with the left foot.

A simple left is a step sideways onto the left foot, then a step to close the right foot to the left. A simple right is a step sideways onto the right foot, then a step to close the left foot to the right.

Doubles

A double consists of three steps and a pieds joints. To perform these sideways you will assume a proper bearing after the révérence of salutation, and, while keeping the right foot firmly in position, throw your left foot out to the side which makes a pieds largis for the first bar. Then for the second bar, keep the left foot firmly in position, bringing the right foot near the left which will make a pieds largis that is almost a pieds joints. For the third bar keep the right foot firm and throw the left foot out to the side which will make a pieds largis, and for the fourth bar keep the left foot firm and bring the right foot close to it which will make a pieds joints.

A double left is a step sideways onto the left foot, a step to almost close the right foot to the left, a step sideways onto the left foot, then a step to close the right foot to the left.

A double right is a step sideways onto the right foot, a step to almost close the left foot to the right, a step sideways onto the right foot, then a step to close the left foot to the right.

This is the basic, or common, version of the step; however, Arbeau gives a number of variations.

Sauts

There is a movement called saut which takes place when both feet are raised in the air and is livelier still. And you should understand that there are two kinds of saut, to whit, saut majeur and petit saut.

Arbeau describes the saut as being a leap. A saut majeur is a big leap in the air, landing with the feet together. A petit saut is a little jump or bounce on the move.

Capriole

While executing the saut majeur they move their feet in the air and such capering is called Capriole.

A capriole consists of a jump in the air while moving the feet backward and forward quickly, followed by a graceful landing (the hard part).

Grève and Pied en l'Air

The dancer throws his weight upon one foot to support his body and raises the other into the air in front of him as if he were about to kick someone. This movement is done in two ways, with the right foot when it is called grève droite and with the left foot when it is called grève gauche. Sometimes the foot is only raised slightly off the ground and moved a little, if at all, forward and this is called pied en l'air droit if the right foot is lifted. . . . The said movement must be performed barely off the ground and gently as a damsel might do it.

This description can be a little confusing, as the other step names generally tell you the direction of travel as well as the foot to start on. For a grève or

pied en l'air, the name tells you which foot to finish the movement with.

For a pied en l'air right, spring onto the left foot, holding the right foot forward, raised a little above the ground. For a grève, kick higher.

For a pied en l'air left, spring onto the right foot, raising the left foot a little above the ground. For a grève, kick higher.

THE DANCES

The Pavan

The pavan . . . is usually danced before the basse dance. The said pavan has not become obsolete or gone out of fashion, nor do I believe it ever will although in truth it is less popular than it was in the past. Our musicians play it when a maiden of good family is taken to Holy Church to be married or when they lead a procession of the chaplains, masters and brethren of some notable confraternity. On solemn feast days the pavan is employed by kings, princes and great noblemen to display themselves in their fine mantles and ceremonial robes. And it is the pavans . . . that announce the grand ball and are arranged to last until the dancers have circled the hall two or three times, unless they prefer to dance it by advancing and retreating.

The pavan is therefore basically a processional dance. As Arbeau says, it can be danced as a processional for the entry of a bride. It could equally well be used as a grand entrance into the hall for the diners at a feast.

Arbeau: "The pavan is easy to dance as it is mearly [sic] two simples and one double forward and two simples and one double backwards. It is played in double time, you will note that the two simples and the double forward are begun with the left foot and the two simples and the double backwards are begun with the right foot."

Capriol: "Then the tabor and other instruments play eight bars while the dancers advance and eight bars while they move backwards."

Arbeau: "That is so, and if one does not wish to move backwards one may continue to advance all the time."

Capriol: "I find these pavans and basse dances charming and dignified, and well suited to honourable persons, particularly ladies and maidens."

The pavan is danced as a long line of couples, with a very simple pattern of stepping, repeating until the music stops:
Simple left, simple right, double left.
Simple right, simple left, double right.
If you wish to make the dance last longer, you can use backward steps; the entire line of dancers can also make turns. As Arbeau says, "Upon approaching the end of the hall you continue to guide the damsel forward while you yourself move backwards as she advances until you are facing the opposite direction from which you started." The music Arbeau gives for the dance is a song.

Branles

Branles, or brawles, as they were known in England, belonged to the middle rung of society, not the court. Some were written for masquerades; others had their origins in the round dances of earlier times or the dances of the French peasantry. Whatever the source, their nature is fairly raucous and their humor earthy, especially in branles performed as mime.

Capriol: "I have noticed that in good society they usually begin the dancing with a branle. Tell me how these should be danced."

Arbeau: ". . . you should understand that the branle is danced by moving sideways and not forward."

Capriol: "I like branles because a number of persons can enjoy them together"

Arbeau: "When you commence a branle several others will join you, as many young men as do damsels, and sometimes the damsel who is the last to arrive will take your left hand and it will thus become a round dance."

Arbeau's descriptions indicate that branles can be danced in a variety of formations, such as lines or circles, and the structure of the dances is fairly loose; the participants can join in at will and turn a line into a circle midway through a dance. This is still true of modern French folk dances, where the band starts playing and people join in when they feel like it, nip off for a glass of wine, and return at will.

Branle Des Pois

Among the branles with mimic gestures is the Pease branle, otherwise known as the Marguerititotte, which is danced in light duple time either like the common branle or the Haut Barrois, as one prefers. Any equal number of men and women take part and they dance it in the manner you will see described in the tabulation which follows.

The Branle Des Pois, or Pease Brawl (meaning peas), is a dance for any number of couples in a circle.

Steps
Everyone joins hands in a ring, then:
Double left, double right, double left, double right; drop hands.
Men only: Saut majeur (women watch amazed)
Women only: Saut majeur (men eye them up)
Men only: step left, then three petit sauts to left.
Women only: Saut majeur.
Men only: Saut majeur.
Women only: Step left, then three petit sauts to left.
Repeat until the dancers or musicians get tired.

Branle de l'Official

The men take the women by the waist and assist them to leap into the air and alight upon the said cadence. Meanwhile the men remain firmly upon both feet to support their partners and are much hindered in these circumstances if they perforce must lift a damsel who will make no effort herself.

"Official" in the title of this branle either refers to the "office"—that is, the household servants—or to an "official," meaning an ecclesiastical judge, a post which the author, Jean Tabourot, held at one point in his career.

Like the Branle Des Pois, this dance is for any number of couples in a circle.

Double left, double right, double left, double right.
Simple left six times.
Pied en l'air right, pied en l'air left, then women
    jump in the air assisted by the men.

A nice variation is for the women to jump across
the men into the next position in the ring. Repeat
until exhausted dancers return to their original
partners.

BRANLE DES POIS

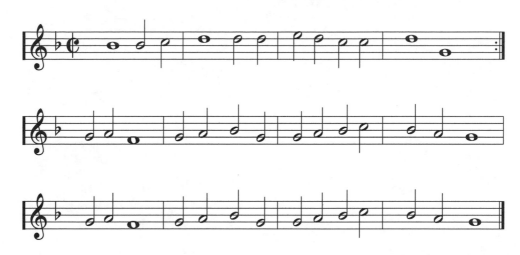

BRANLE DE L'OFFICIAL

BELLE QUI TIENS MA VIE

1. Fair one, who holds my heart
   Captive within thine eyes,
   Whose gracious smiles impart
   Secrets of Paradise
   Give me hope to cherish
   For without I perish

2. Fly not, I entreat thee,
   For in thy presence fair
   I am lost completely
   To myself and care.
   Thy divine perfection
   claims my whole affection.

3. Such grace of form and face
   Kindles a sweet desire,
   My icy heart yields place
   To a heart all afire,
   Fanned by ardent yearning
   Passionately burning.

4. I wandered fancy free,
   Nor glance nor sigh I gave
   Till love imprisoned me,
   And I became his slave,
   Ready to die for him,
   Sworn to his slightest whim.

5. Draw near, O mistress mine,
   Come closer to me still.
   Since I am wholly thine
   Soften thy rebel will,
   Mend my heart with the bliss
   of one sweet healing kiss.

6. Angel, my life's eclipse,
   In thine embrace I die.
   The honey of thy lips
   Sweetens my parting sigh,
   And my soul soars above
   Borne on the wings of love.

7. Oceans shall surge no more
   And heaven's eye wax cold
   Full many a moon before
   My love for thee grows old,
   Or wanes a single jot
   If thou forsake me not.

CHAPTER 15
COSTUMES AND CLOTHING

◆

No single element will add more to the authenticity of your medieval event than attractive costumes. Somehow, putting on the costume of a far-removed time and place alters not only our perception of ourselves and each other but, unless we actually fight against it, also our behavior. Simply put, if you look medieval, you are more likely to feel and act medieval.

That's the easy part. The hard part is getting all your guests appropriately dressed, so before we discuss costume styles and patterns, there are a few facts about costumes you need to consider. First, if your medieval feast is a private function, either by invitation or paid subscription, you have every right to insist that anyone who attends wear a costume. However, unless your friends and guests are all very enlightened, or really good sports, there will be dangers in demanding that everyone wear a costume. Some will dress up grudgingly, but they may get into the mood when they see everyone else is in costume, too. Others will simply refuse to come in costume.

If, on the other hand, your feast is a public or semi-public affair, be it a church-sponsored Twelfth Night feast or a wedding, there is absolutely no way you are going to persuade everyone to come in costume. It won't happen, and there is nothing you can do about it, so don't worry. If you examine the wedding photos in this book, you will almost inevitably see people in modern clothes. Encourage everyone as much as possible, but understand it will have limited effect. If the event is repeated annually, you will find that repeat visitors will slowly come around to wearing costumes. Chances are that anyone who returns more than a second time is likely to be in costume. Whatever the case, for the medieval experience to be completely effective, proper costumes are important. Dancing the pavan or enjoying a sumptuous feast in T-shirt and jeans or a business suit simply doesn't work.

With these limitations in mind, let us move on to discussing medieval dress. Having decided that everyone should attend in costume, the big question is how to find the right look. The easy answer is to rent them from a costume shop. There is, however, a downside to rented costumes. Unless you are in a major metropolitan area where there are companies that rent costumes to professional theaters and movie companies, the selection of medieval clothing is likely to be severely limited and pretty tacky. Besides, a lot of the other guests will want to rent their costumes, and if there are none left to rent, they might give up. This leaves you with either making your own or having it made for you. You may even persuade a circle of friends to help make costumes for a core group of guests. In any case, there remains the question of style and patterns.

Medieval fashion changed almost as rapidly as modern styles. Every generation, an entirely new look became popular. Naturally, the ability to keep up with the latest fashion trend depended on where you lived and how much disposable income you had available. Since the period of our feast is roughly the mid-fourteenth century (around 1350), and most of our food, music, and customs have come from England and France, we will concentrate on clothing styles from that place and time, and limit our wardrobe to the upper-middle ranks of society.

Some of you are skilled enough, especially with the simplistic construction techniques used during the Middle Ages, to make costumes solely on the basis of the illustrations scattered throughout this book or in the costume books listed in the bibliography. Others will need full-scale patterns, available from the pattern companies listed in the sources at the end of this book. Still others will need some guidance but not fully detailed patterns. To those of you who fall into this last category, we dedicate the remainder of this chapter. Good luck.

To make medieval clothing construction easy to digest, we will break the general category of clothing into bite-size pieces. First, understand that medieval clothing did share one thing with modern clothes: Many of the same items were worn by both men and women. Today it is T-shirt and jeans; then it was kirtles and surcoats. We will start by identifying the types of materials you will be using, and then take the basic garments one by one, beginning with the undergarments and working our way out.

FABRIC

Fabric made seven hundred years ago was heavier than today's clothing fabric. For most of the clothes in this chapter, it is better to use upholstery fabric than clothing fabric; not only is it more authentic, but the heavier-weight fabrics will allow the clothes to hang right. Medieval fabric colors tended to be rich and vibrant; pastels were unknown. Deep reds, deep blue, emerald green, ocher, bright yellow, and chocolate brown were worn by both sexes. Ladies might wear deep pink, soft blue, or light green, but that was about as far from the primary color scheme as anybody got. Colors were mixed freely. An emerald green gown might be lined with bright gold and worn over deep blue hose. The most elaborate and expensive material was reserved for the cotehardie, the main outergarment. Here, fine velvets, brocades, and damasks were common. Stripes, dots, and small patterns were virtually unknown, and although diamond patterns did exist, they were of a very large scale, the diamonds usually four to five inches in height. Tartans were worn only by Scottish people.

BUTTONS

The fourteenth century saw the introduction of the first buttons. Unlike today's flat buttons, fourteenth-century buttons were generally tiny balls of cloth stuffed with wool. To achieve a similar effect, use small, round, pea-size buttons.

KIRTLE

Normally made of lightweight material, the kirtle was the basic medieval undergarment. The only thing worn under the kirtle was hose. The kirtle was worn by both sexes. Women's were universally long, while men's were a variety of lengths, depending on whether the man was wearing a long or short cotehardie over it. If the kirtle is going to be entirely covered by an overgarment, the kirtle can be made of nothing more exotic than lightweight linen or cotton, though cotton was unknown in medieval Europe. If, on the other hand, the overgarment has a low-cut collar or open sleeves that allow part of the kirtle to show, then the kirtle should be made of a better-quality material, either heavy linen or upholstery-weight silk or satin. Virtually all kirtles were a single color. Men's were frequently white, but women's might be any color at all. Because little of the kirtle is seen, its construction can be extremely simple.

CHAUSES

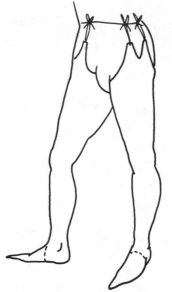

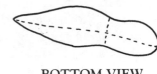

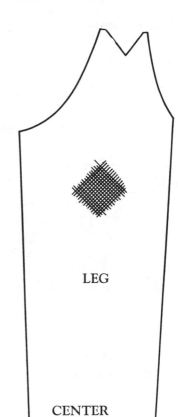

**BOTTOM VIEW
SHOWING SEAMS**

LEG

CENTER
POINT

TOE

KIRTLE

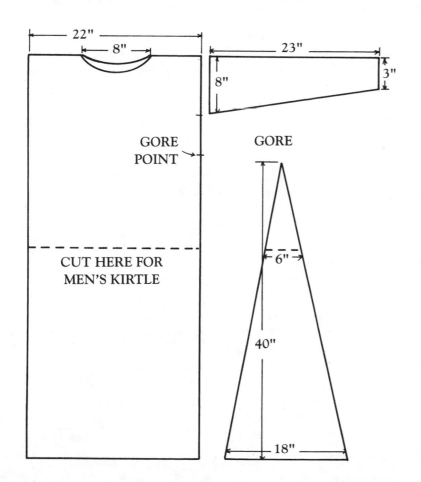

22"

8"

23"

8"

3"

GORE
POINT

GORE

6"

40"

18"

CUT HERE FOR
MEN'S KIRTLE

The pattern shows a kirtle twenty-two inches wide. This should serve for most slim to medium-size people; for the more ample figure, the pattern will have to be adjusted to a comfortable fit.

Fold the material across the shoulders so both front and back can be cut from the same piece of fabric. The length will be determined by the sex of the wearer. Men's kirtles generally stop four to five inches below the waist, unless they will be wearing a very short cotehardie, in which case the kirtles should be adjusted accordingly. Women's kirtles, on the other hand, should hang to the ankle. Cut the neck opening, making sure it falls slightly lower in the front than in the back. Next, cut two gores as shown in the illustration. For slim males, the insertion of a gore may not be necessary, but even the slimmest ladies will need the gore to allow free movement of the legs.

Sew the sides of the kirtle from the bottom of the arm opening to the top of the gore, and sew the gores in place. Turn the kirtle inside out so the seams are on the inside. Have the wearer try on the body of the kirtle to make sure the arm openings are large enough, and set the hem line. Hem the bottom and neck. In one surviving medieval kirtle, the neck line is overlaid with a simple bias tape to provide an attractive finished edge.

Check the arm length of the wearer against the suggested arm length in the illustration. Fold the arms across the top so both the front and back of the arms can be cut from one piece of fabric. Cut the arms and sew the bottom seam, stopping about three inches above the wrist. Hem both sides of the three-inch opening to form a vent, similar to those found on modern shirts.

Turn both the kirtle and sleeves inside out, and sew the arms into the arm openings. Have the wearer put on the kirtle to check the length of the sleeves. They should be about one inch longer than the sleeves on a modern shirt. Adjust the length as necessary. The cuff may be closed either with one or two small buttons, similar to a modern shirt, or by sewing a small pocket into the cuff hem through which a drawstring can be run. The drawstring can then simply be pulled snug and tied in a bow.

CHAUSES

Chauses were leggings, not really tights in the way we think of them today, but more like heavy socks that went up to the crotch. We have provided a pattern for a pair of chauses, but it is far simpler to buy a pair of heavyweight dance tights. If you want to look really fashionable, buy two pairs and cut them in half along the crotch seam, reassembling them so that the left and right legs are different colors.

Ladies' hose were no more than a short version of men's chauses, secured at the knee with a pair of garters. Again, it is just as easy to use a pair of dance tights, or even knee-length hose or socks in a bright, plain color.

If you decide you want to make your own chauses, they will have to be custom fit to each individual pair of legs, because they are made from nonstretch fabric. Following the pattern for the main leg section, cut a rough pattern from soft cloth, such as an old sheet. Fit the pattern around the leg, making sure the tie points fall two to three inches below the waist. Next, fit the hose around the leg, pinning it in position at the center back of the leg. Trim off the excess fabric, allowing a quarter-inch overlap. Leave enough material that the sides can be tucked under the foot far enough to overlap at least half an inch. Cut out the horseshoe-shaped area to fit comfortably across the top of the foot.

When the pattern fits comfortably, transfer it to the final cloth, making sure the weave of the fabric is on the bias—that is, the weave should run at a forty-five-degree angle to the pattern (see the small area in the illustration showing how the weave should lie). It is historically correct to make the legs different colors and is an appropriately splashy fashion statement.

Turn the legging inside out, sew up the rear seam, and hem around the top, after making sure the tie points fall so that one is on the side of the body and the other in front of the hip. Put the legging back on the person who will be wearing it. Tuck the ends under the foot, and trim them so they overlap about a quarter inch and conform neatly around the heel. Turn the legging inside out once again, and sew the two sides of the heel together and around the back of the heel.

Shape the toe piece around the foot, and trim it so the bottom seam overlaps a quarter inch and the back end of the toe fits comfortably under the opening in the leg. Mark around the front edge of the legging where it rests on the toe. Trim any excess material from the toe as necessary, sew the two sides of the toe together, and attach the toe to the legging. The seam where the toe joins the legging can be seen in the main illustration, and the seams on the bottom of the foot are shown in the small illustration of the bottom of the foot. Be sure that any seams beneath the foot lie flat so they do not make the wearer uncomfortable when walking.

Since there is no crotch in the chauses, the wearer will still have to wear underpants. We suggest a pair of bicycle shorts, because they are sturdy enough to allow the tie points to be pinned fast without tearing the shorts or pulling them down when the wearer sits. Alternatively, a soft cloth belt can be tied around the waist and attached to the chauses by means of string or ribbon ties as shown in the main illustration.

Ladies' chauses are essentially the same as men's, except that they only go up to the knee, where they are held in place with a ribbon or garter.

COTEHARDIE

As the primary outergarment, the cotehardie was made from the most sumptuous material the wearer could afford. The best material to use for your cotehardie is either a damask or velvet upholstery-weight fabric. A large, diamond-shaped pattern (a harlequin print) is appropriately medieval but will prove very hard to find. Upholstery fabric with a small pattern can be used but is not as authentically medieval as a larger pattern. The cotehardie was always lined, usually in a plain color, often in silk if the wearer could afford it.

Women's cotehardies were universally floor-length, sometimes with a train that might extend one to four feet behind the gown—lovely to look at, but a little clumsy if you are not used to them. Men's cotehardies varied tremendously. Some were extremely form-fitting affairs that ended at the crotch (most popular among young men with good legs); others were full-cut, floor-length versions (more popular among mature or slightly overweight guys). There were also knee-length and mid-calf-length versions.

Sleeve styles and lengths varied as much as the hemline. Some cotehardies had very tight sleeves; others had long, flowing sleeves that hung below the knee. If the sleeves were full, the tighter-fitting sleeves of the kirtle beneath would show. The front edge of these large sleeves was often ornamented in some way. It might be trimmed in fur or cut into decorative dags, examples of which are given below. If a man was wearing a knee- or mid-calf-length cotehardie, the hem might be cut in dags to match the sleeves.

There are three basic styles shown in the illustrations: the men's short cotehardie, the men's long cotehardie (later called a houppelande), and a women's cotehardie. Any of the four sleeve styles is appropriate with any of the bodies. Similarly, the men's short

cotehardie is shown with a high collar, which can also be used with the longer version. With the variety of patterns provided, you can mix and match an almost endless variety of styles, depending on your personal taste.

Men's Short Cotehardie. This most form-fitting of medieval garments is made from four identical sections, each making up one-quarter of the coat: front left, front right, back left, and back right. The only difference between the front and back panels is that the neck opening drops slightly lower in the front. The cotehardie in the illustration is sized for a man about five foot, ten in height, with a forty-inch chest and thirty-two-inch waist. Since the wearer may differ from this, we advise making cloth patterns and fitting them first. Make the pattern in four sections, and pin the back sections together, allowing one inch extra where they will be sewn together. Pin the front panels to the sides, but do not pin them together at the front seam until the wearer has gotten into the pattern.

When the pattern is on the wearer, adjust the side and back seams to be relatively form-fitting. Allow the front sections to overlap sufficiently to install buttonholes and buttons. Do not make the cotehardie fit too tightly; it should fit slightly tighter than a suit coat, but no tighter than a loose vest or waistcoat. It can be more form-fitting on slim men than on stouter ones. To allow the body of the garment to fit across the hips, you will probably have to add a small gore between the side panels. The gore and its proper location are shown in the illustration. If the wearer has very small hips, the gore may not be necessary, but he has to be able to sit down without tearing the side seams. If you prefer not to use a gore, a vent on either side will allow the same ease of movement.

After marking the seam locations on the pattern, disassemble the pattern, and cut the segments of the garment from the final fabric. To add interest to the cotehardie, consider making the front left and rear right panels one color and the front right and rear left another.

Before assembling the four sections of the body, install inner facings along both sides of the front closure. This will provide support for the buttons and buttonholes. Pin the sections together so the garment is inside out, and sew them together. Stop the side seams three inches below the arm opening. When the arm is attached, you will have to insert a gusset at this point. When the cotehardie has been assembled, fit it on the wearer to make final adjustments to the fit and

MEN'S SHORT COTEHARDIE

MANTLE

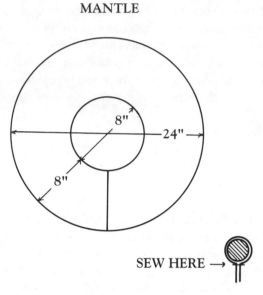

8"

24"

8"

SEW HERE →

WELTING
(CROSS SECTION)

COLLAR

15"

2"

3"

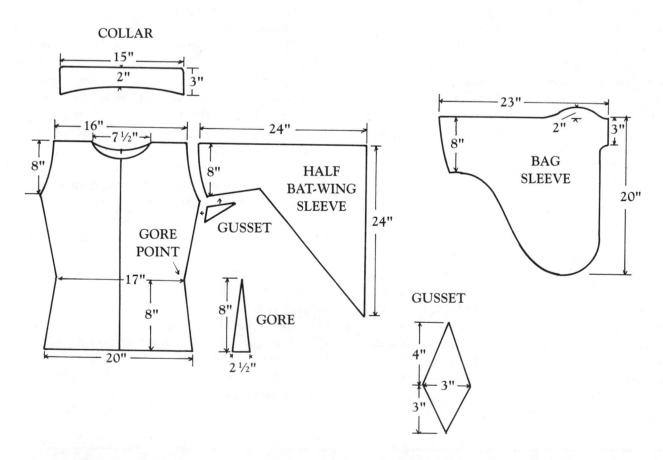

16"

7 ½"

24"

8"

8"

HALF
BAT-WING
SLEEVE

24"

GUSSET

GORE
POINT

17"

8"

8"

GORE

2 ½"

23"

2"

3"

8"

BAG
SLEEVE

20"

GUSSET

4"

3"

3"

20"

122

find the proper hem length. This can vary according to taste from just below the crotch to mid-calf, depending on how much leg you want to show. If you want to decorate the hem with dags, there are a variety of styles illustrated later in this chapter.

The sleeves can be made from one or two pieces of cloth. To make them from a single piece, fold the fabric in two along the top line of the arm before cutting around the outline of the sleeve. When the sleeves are set into the body of the cotehardie, be sure they taper into the armhole on the body. To ensure ease of movement, insert a gusset into the underside of the sleeve. The long dimension (four inches) of the gusset is set into the seam on the bottom of the sleeve, and the short dimension (three inches) into the side seam of the body. A detail of this gusset, and its positioning on the garment, is shown in the illustration.

Though we have shown the collar fashionably high, the exact height of your collar depends on the taste and neck length of the wearer. The collar is simple to make. Just cut two identical pieces as shown and a third from a stiff lining material to give the collar rigidity. Lay the outside faces of the collar material together, place the lining material on top, sew around the edges, and turn it inside out. Then, attach the collar around the neck of the surcoat. The collar need not meet in front. Ideally, to make the garment hang right, it should be fully lined, but this is left to your discretion.

Mantle. The mantle was a shoulder-length cloak worn as much for decorative effect as for warmth. The mantle in the illustration of the young man in a short cotehardie shows a garment that is no more than a variation on the hood and liripipe. In this instance, the mantle has been used to its best decorative effect by ornamenting the edges with dags that match those on the sleeves.

The mantle is no more than a circle of cloth two feet in diameter, with an eight-inch-diameter hole in the center and a front opening so it can be tied around the neck rather than pulled on over the head. To give the mantle enough body to hang properly, it should be lined. The lining may be of any matching, contrasting, or coordinating fabric, but if the mantle is designed to be worn with a specific cotehardie, we suggest reversing the color scheme of the cotehardie in the mantle. For example, if the cotehardie is blue velvet lined in gold satin, the mantle should be of gold velvet lined in blue satin.

An additional air of sophistication can be added to the mantle by finishing the collar with a thick welting. Similar to the welting used around the edges of sofa cushions, tailor's welting is no more than a layer of cloth sewn around a length of soft rope. Cut a length of three-eighths- or half-inch soft cotton rope to the length of the circumference of the neck opening—in this case, about twenty-five inches. Cut a strip of the same cloth as the outer surface of the mantle. The strip should be two inches longer than the rope, an inch and three quarters wide, and cut on the bias. Wrap the cloth over the rope, and sew it in place as shown in the welting cross-section illustration. The ends of the rope are covered by tucking the ends of the cloth around the ends of the rope and sewing them in place. Insert the welting between the outer fabric and the lining, and sew it in place.

Men's Full-length Cotehardie (Houppelande). The men's full-length cotehardie is a longer, fuller version of the short one. The body is made from two pieces of fabric, rather than four, and is cut fuller across the chest to allow it to flow better. Two variations of the body are shown in the illustrations. Variation 1 is for use with a patternless cloth, such as velvet. If you are constructing this version of the garment, you have the choice of two methods of adding fullness to the gown and providing ease of movement. The main illustration shows the gown with gores inset in the front and rear, and the side seams left open from mid-hip to the floor. (This version is designed for the man who may no longer be young, but is still proud enough of his legs that he doesn't mind showing them off.)

A variant of this design is achieved by installing gores into the sides as well as the front and rear of the garment. If four gores are used, the individual gores are narrower than if only two gores are used.

Variation 2 provides a pattern for a cotehardie made with a damask-type material. Because it is impossible to inset a gore and keep the pattern consistent, the only way to provide the necessary fullness is to make the front and rear sections of the garment wider at the bottom. In this instance, you still have the option of leaving the side seams open, as shown in the main illustration, or sewing them closed. If the wearer has a stocky build, you have the option of setting a gore in the back of the gown. Although the pattern will not match where the gore is set in, the natural folds and pleats that form at the back of the cotehardie when it is belted will nearly hide the irregularities.

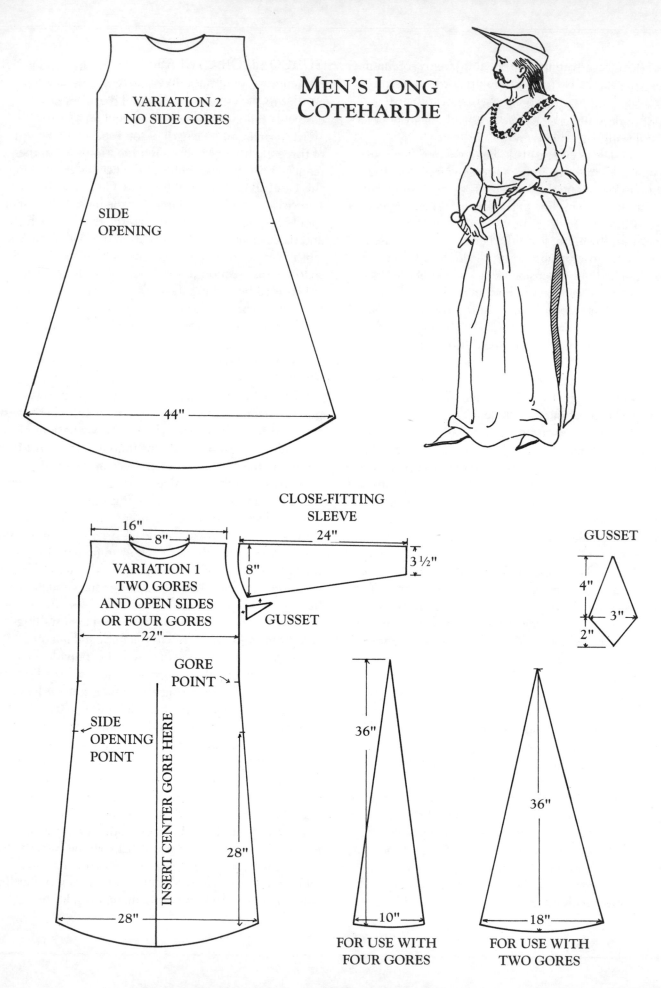

MEN'S LONG COTEHARDIE

VARIATION 2
NO SIDE GORES

SIDE
OPENING

44"

CLOSE-FITTING
SLEEVE

16"

8"

VARIATION 1
TWO GORES
AND OPEN SIDES
OR FOUR GORES

22"

24"

8"

3 ½"

GUSSET

GUSSET

4"

3"

2"

GORE
POINT

SIDE
OPENING
POINT

INSERT CENTER GORE HERE

28"

36"

36"

28"

10"

18"

FOR USE WITH
FOUR GORES

FOR USE WITH
TWO GORES

Whichever variation of the full-length cotehardie you choose, the bottom of the skirt is cut in a semi-circular shape. This allows the garment to hang properly and provides you with enough material to adjust the hem with no danger of the gown being too short in the front or rear. Properly, the full-length cotehardie should drag slightly on the ground, as shown in the main illustration. Walking in a gown of this length may take some practice. If you wish, make the hem slightly shorter so there is no danger of the wearer tripping.

The arms shown with this version of the cotehardie are constructed and set in place in the same manner as on the short-skirted version described above. Because the gown itself is fuller, the short end of the gusset can be made slightly smaller than in the short cotehardie. Any sleeve style is appropriate, and a collar is optional.

Women's Cotehardie. The women's cotehardie is very similar to the men's full-length version. The main differences lie in the neckline and the fullness of the body. The neck is wider than on the men's cotehardie, being open enough that it just rests on the edges of the shoulder. As in all cases, the front of the neckline should be cut slightly lower than the back. When cutting the neck, take care not to make it too large; the weight of the gown can easily cause the dress to pull off one or both shoulders. The skirt begins to widen immediately beneath the arms to give more room to the bust and make the entire garment more graceful and flowing. The rear panel is cut slightly longer than the front to provide some natural train, which can be accentuated by insetting an extended gore. Even if no additional train is desired, a rear gore the same length as the rest of the gown will make the cotehardie more full and attractive.

For the fuller-figured woman, or for those who simply want a more flowing look, gores can also be added at the side seams. Note in the illustration that the side gores are only inserted from the waistline.

Again, the sleeves in the women's cotehardie can be adapted from any of the four styles shown. If you elect to use the bat-wing sleeve shown in the illustration, be sure to insert the gusset. Even though the sleeve itself is very full, the arm opening is only eight inches in diameter and will require a gusset if the arm is to move freely. The sleeves can be ornamented with decorative trim, as shown in the main illustration, or cut into decorative dags.

SURCOAT, OR CYCLAS

The surcoat, or cyclas, was an extra layer of clothes worn over the cotehardie. Men's surcoats were generally no more than coats without sleeves; as with modern coats, some were made of fabric, some of leather. In either case, the lines were relatively simple. Women's surcoats tended to be longer and generally had vastly larger arm openings than those worn by men, allowing glimpses of the female form, wrapped in a close-fitting cotehardie (or occasionally just a fine silk kirtle), to be seen moving inside the surcoat. Generally, though not always, the surcoat was made from plain fabric, the more elaborate fabric of the cotehardie being exposed at the arms and along the bottom hem. To add luxury to the otherwise relatively plain surcoat, the hem, armholes, and neck were sometimes trimmed in fur, and sometimes the body of the surcoat was painted or embroidered with the family coat of arms.

Women's Surcoat. The women's surcoat is extremely simple in construction, but must be fitted to the individual wearer in order to hang right and still keep its shape. Because the surcoat was often considered a winter garment, it should be made of fairly heavy material. A lining will help it move properly but is entirely optional.

The body of the surcoat is made from identical front and back pieces, as shown in the illustration. The only points where the front is attached to the back are at the shoulders, the few inches between the side opening at the hip line, and the openings where the side gores are inset. It will be wise to make a pattern out of soft cloth, such as an old sheet, and tailor the neck and side openings to fit the wearer. Measurements such as the width across the hips will vary considerably, depending on the individual. The surcoat should not fit tightly but should move easily over the garments underneath. Be sure the side openings fall to the point of the hips, as shown on the figure in the main illustration. The outer edge of the shoulder should rest just at the point of the wearer's shoulder. The depth of the neckline depends on the bustline of the wearer.

When you are satisfied that the pattern fits the wearer, cut the front and back sections of the surcoat, slit the panels to receive the front and rear gores, and sew the two panels together at shoulder and hips. Next, insert the gores at the front, back, and sides. Then hem around the neck and arm openings. The surcoat can vary in length, from dragging on the floor to

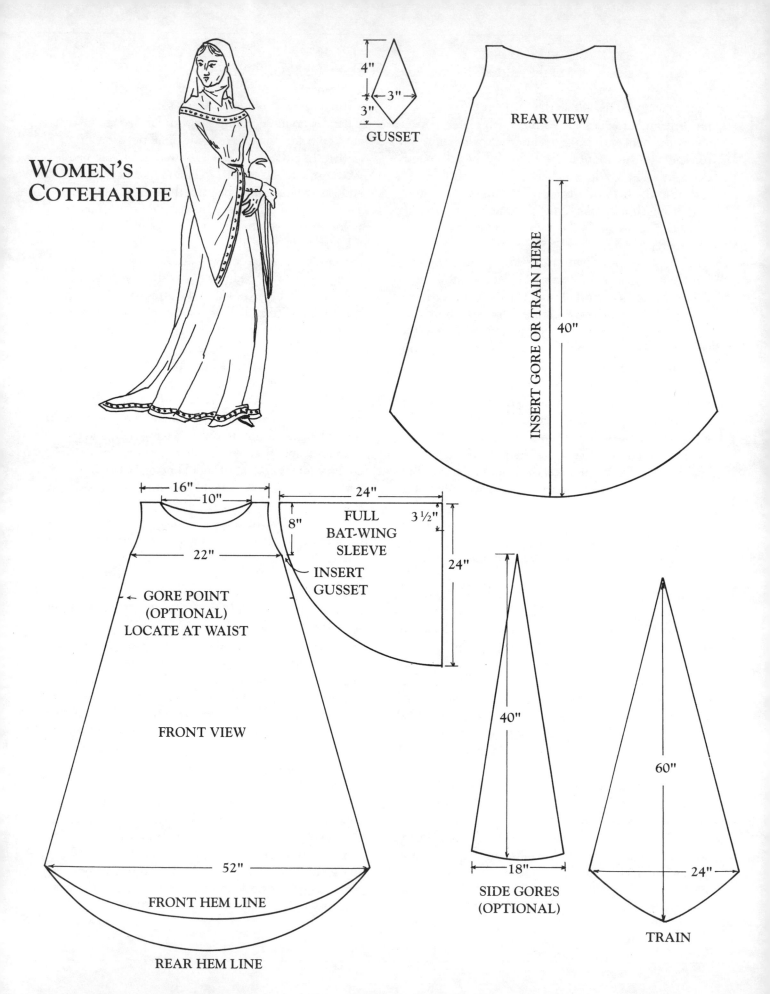

WOMEN'S COTEHARDIE

GUSSET

4"
3"
3"

REAR VIEW

INSERT GORE OR TRAIN HERE

40"

16"
10"
22"

24"

8"

FULL BAT-WING SLEEVE

3½"

24"

GORE POINT (OPTIONAL) LOCATE AT WAIST

INSERT GUSSET

FRONT VIEW

52"

FRONT HEM LINE

REAR HEM LINE

40"

18"

SIDE GORES (OPTIONAL)

60"

24"

TRAIN

126

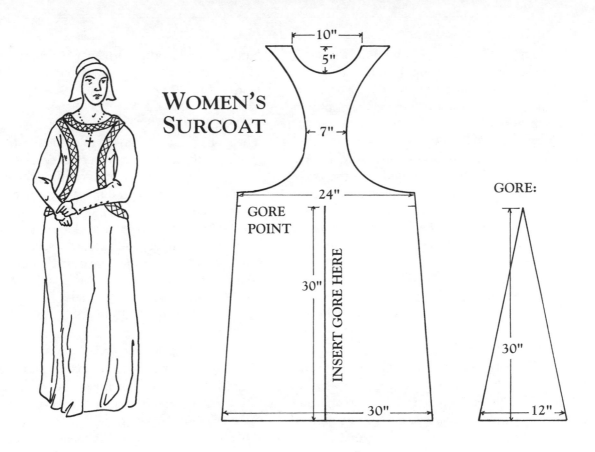

WOMEN'S SURCOAT

10"

5"

7"

GORE:

GORE POINT

24"

30"

INSERT GORE HERE

30"

30"

12"

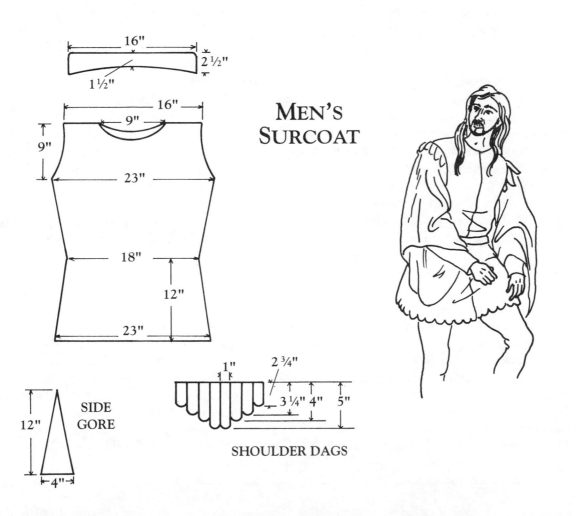

16"

2 ½"

1 ½"

16"

9"

9"

23"

MEN'S SURCOAT

18"

12"

23"

12"

SIDE GORE

4"

1"

2 ¾"

3 ¼" 4" 5"

SHOULDER DAGS

allowing five to six inches of the cotehardie to show beneath the hem; it is entirely up to your taste. Additional interest can be added by sewing decorative trim or fur around the neck and side openings, as shown in the main illustration.

Men's Surcoat. The men's surcoat is very similar in construction to the men's short cotehardie. Follow the instructions for the short cotehardie for the basic construction, but as an overgarment, the surcoat must be large enough to fit over the cotehardie. Some men's surcoats were pulled on over the head, while others buttoned up the front. The surcoat in the main illustration is pulled over the head. If yours is going to follow this design, it must be even looser-fitting than one that is buttoned. Note that the large, loose sleeves in the main illustration are part of the cotehardie, not the surcoat.

Make the pattern in four sections, as you did with the cotehardie, but if the surcoat is going to be worn over the head, pin the front sections together, as well as the sides and back. Put the pattern on the wearer, and adjust the seams for a comfortable fit, keeping in mind the amount of clothing that will be worn underneath. Be sure the surcoat can be taken off without removing any of the pins. This should be no problem if it has a button front, but if it's a pullover, it needs to fit fairly loosely.

When the coat has been assembled, fit it on the wearer and find the proper hem length. The main illustration shows the surcoat at mid-thigh, which is the length in the pattern. You may decide to decorate the hem with dags, such as those shown in the picture. Alternative dag styles are shown later in this chapter. If you decide to add dags to the bottom, or even if you don't, you may want to consider the interesting shoulder dags shown in the illustration. A pattern for these is provided here. It is best if the individual dags are made separately. Each dag should be lined with a matching or contrasting material. Sew the dag and lining together, turn inside out to hide the seamed edge, and attach to the body of the surcoat. The two longest dags should go on either side of the shoulder seam, with the shorter progressing down the front and back of the arm opening. They should come down no farther than those shown in the main illustration.

To add interest, consider painting the surcoat with your coat of arms. You can make it entirely from leather for a huntsman or woodsman look. Another option is the addition of a collar, but the collar on the surcoat should not come as high as that on the cote-

hardie. As with other garments, the surcoat should be fully lined, unless it is the work garment of a woodsman, but this is up to you.

MONK'S ROBE
The monk's robe was a very traditional garment similar to those previously worn in secular society by both sexes. By the fourteenth century, these long tunics were pretty much limited to members of the clergy. Ecclesiastical tunics were universally made of heavy-weight, coarsely woven cloth in gray, black, white, or brown, depending on the specific order of the monk. Monk's cloth was very coarsely woven; select your fabric accordingly. The waist of the tunic was cinched with a belt, usually made of hemp rope. The rope was wrapped twice around the body and knotted in the front. The ends of the belt were allowed to hang to mid-calf length. One end of the belt rope had three knots tied in it three or four inches apart, the knots symbolizing the Holy Trinity of Father, Son, and Holy Spirit. A large rosary was usually tucked into the belt. All monks wore cowls, or hoods. Some were attached to the tunic, but most were a separate piece of clothing. The monks' cowls, like the robes, were much looser fitting than the more fashionable secular model. Directions for making a cowl are in the section on headgear.

Far from form-fitting, monk's habits were loose and baggy, so with slight adjustments to the hem and sleeve length, one size should fit nearly anyone. The body of the gown can be cut from a single length of cloth folded over at the shoulder line. To be sure you have enough length to adjust for the height of the wearer, begin with a piece of cloth ten feet in length, folded over on itself to make a double-thick piece five feet long. Lay out the basic lines of the habit as shown in the illustration. Check that the neck opening falls slightly lower in the front than in the back. Sew the sides of the gown from the front edge of the sleeves to the point where the side gores will be inserted, as illustrated. Next, cut two gores and sew them into the openings at the sides of the gown. Turn the gown inside out so the seams are hidden on the inside.

Have the wearer try on the gown, and mark the hem line so it falls to the ankle. Turn the hem to the inside of the gown and sew. To allow the gown to flow properly, allow a wide, double-turned hem. You may also hem around the neck.

Next, cut four of the sleeve sections shown in the illustration. Depending upon the length of the wearer's

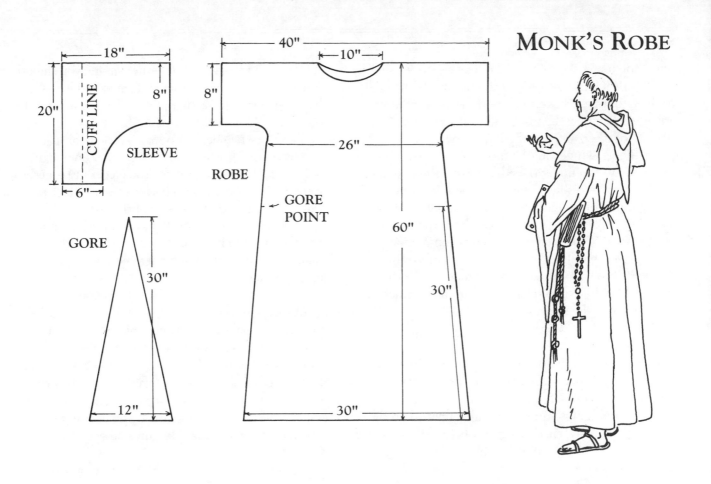

MONK'S ROBE

18"

20"

CUFF LINE

8"

6"

SLEEVE

GORE

30"

12"

40"

10"

8"

ROBE

26"

GORE
POINT

60"

30"

30"

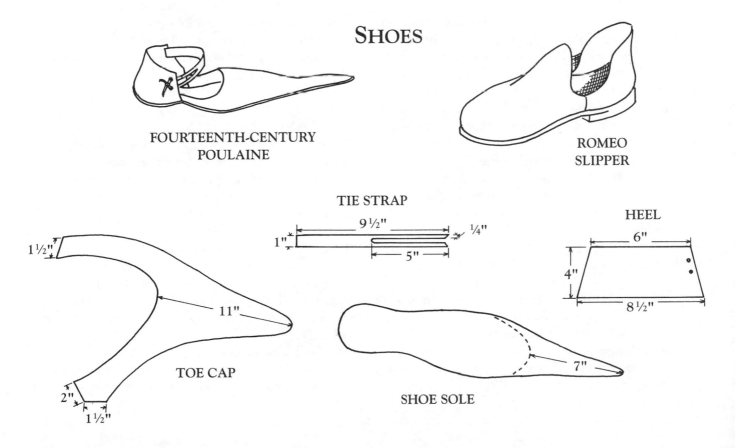

SHOES

FOURTEENTH-CENTURY
POULAINE

ROMEO
SLIPPER

TIE STRAP

9½"

¼"

1"

5"

HEEL

6"

4"

8½"

1½"

11"

2"

1½"

TOE CAP

7"

SHOE SOLE

arms, you may have to make the sleeve sections slightly longer or shorter. The ends of the sleeves should come to the ends of the fingertips when the wearer's arms are extended. Sew the front and back sections of the sleeves together, and sew them into the body of the gown. The gown needn't be turned inside out to do this; simply turn under the edges of the arm openings on the gown and slide the ends of the sleeves inside the opening, pinning them in place before stitching. To adjust the length of the sleeves, have the wearer put on the gown, and turn back the cuffs approximately at the position of the dotted line in the illustration. The cuffs should be three to four inches in depth and ideally should be turned back twice to add fullness and weight to the sleeves.

SHOES
Available in a variety of styles, the most fashionable fourteenth-century shoes were long, pointed affairs known as poulaines. Sometimes the toes reached more than a foot in length and were pulled upward on the end by a chain attached to a garter below the knee (we don't advise you try walking in these). All fourteenth-century shoes had soft soles, making them little more than slippers. When people went outside, they frequently wore pattens, sandals with wooden soles two or three inches thick, over their shoes. Since there is no way to turn out a pair of medieval shoes quickly, unless you are good at leather work, we suggest wearing a pair of hard-soled slippers, such as Romeo slippers, shown in the illustration. Romeos have a semicircular elastic inset on the sides, which can be cut out if you want the shoe to look more authentic. For those of you who are daring, we have included a pattern.

The poulaine was not only the most fashionable shoe of the fourteenth century, it was also the simplest to construct. Begin by making a pattern for the sole by standing on a piece of light cardboard and tracing around your foot. Allow an extra three-eighths inch all around the edge so you can sew the shoe together without losing any foot room. Now extend the toe forward six or seven inches; this will give you enough toe to look impressive, but it will be short enough to navigate.

When the pattern has been cut, trace a left and right sole onto a piece of leather about three-sixteenths inch thick, or use two thicknesses of thinner leather. If you use a single piece of thick leather, the smooth side of the leather should be the bottom surface of the sole. If you use two thinner pieces, cut them so they can be placed rough sides together, giving you smooth surfaces on both the bottom and inner surfaces. Glue these together with leather glue before sewing the shoe together.

Next, cut two heel sections, two tie straps, and two toe pieces from leather slightly less than one-eighth inch thick. To ensure that the toe pieces fit properly over your foot, first make a pattern from a piece of heavy cloth. Stand on the sole of the shoe, and lay the toe pattern over your foot. It should drape comfortably over the foot and hang down far enough on the sides to allow the toe to be sewn onto the sole without making the shoe too tight.

Sew the toe piece onto the sole, keeping the seam about three-sixteenths inch from the outside edge of the sole and making the stitches about a quarter inch in length. The best way to sew these multiple layers of leather together is with the help of a sewing awl. When the front of the shoe is sewn together, sew the heel piece onto the sole, making sure it overlaps the back edges of the toe piece by at least a quarter inch. With both pieces sewn to the sole, run side seams to join the heel and toe pieces.

Finally, position the narrow tie strap on the inner face of the heel, so that when the ties are brought across the shoe, they will be facing the outside of your foot. Sew the tie strap in place. Punch two small holes in the side of the shoe so the ends of the tie strap can be drawn through and tied in a knot or bow, as shown in the picture of the completed poulaine.

Monks wore sandals, no matter what the weather. Modern sandals will be fine as long as they are made from leather and are simple in design.

HATS AND HEADGEAR
No member of proper medieval society would ever go out in public without some form of headgear. Men's and women's hats came in a wide variety of styles, but the most universally popular among the working classes was the hood. Men's hoods tended to be more elaborate than women's, having a long tail known as a liripipe. These might be no more than a foot in length or might drag on the floor; the longer the liripipe, the greater the fashion statement. Next to the hood, women of all stations wore a wimple and veil, an arrangement still seen on members of conservative orders of nuns.

Hood with Liripipe. The hood can either be cut from a single piece of cloth and folded along the top seam or made from two halves sewn together. For the

HOODS AND HATS

HOOD WITH
LIRIPIPE

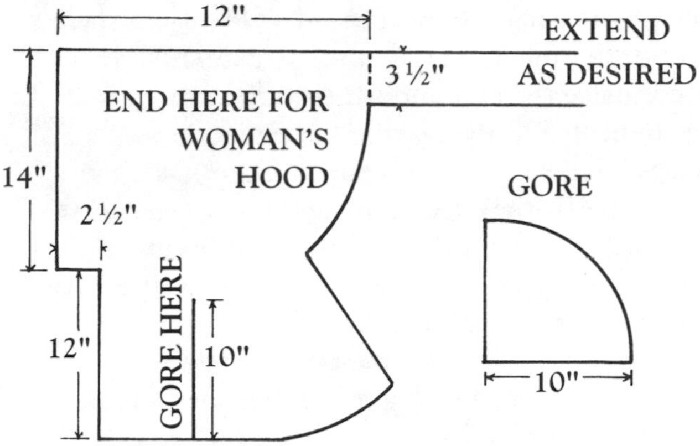

12"

EXTEND
AS DESIRED

3½"

END HERE FOR
WOMAN'S
HOOD

14"

GORE

2½"

GORE HERE

12"

10"

10"

LIRIPIPE WRAPPED
AROUND HEAD

MONK'S
COWL

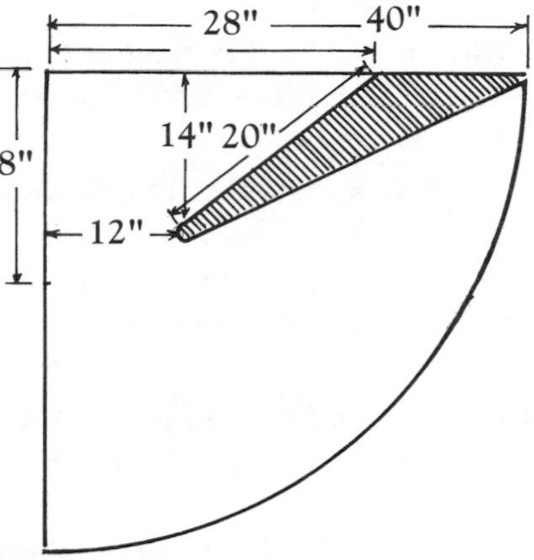

WOMAN WITH
HOOD OPEN

28"

40"

14" 20"

18"

12"

ROBIN HOOD
HAT

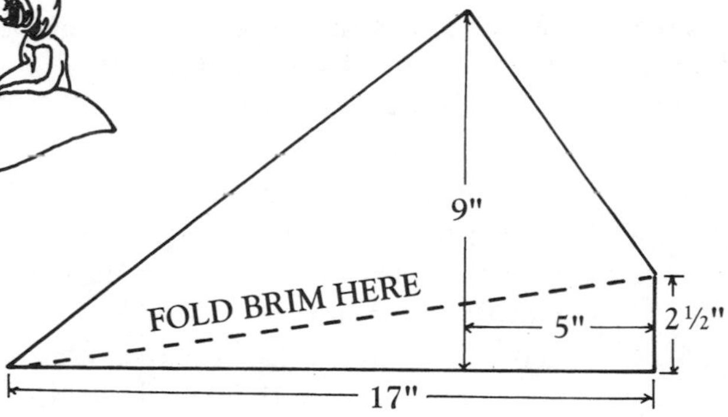

9"

CONE

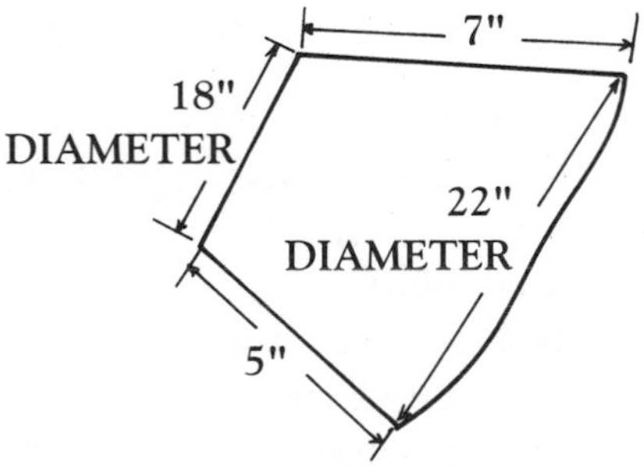

7"

18"
DIAMETER

FOLD BRIM HERE

5"

2½"

22"
DIAMETER

17"

5"

APPET

3"

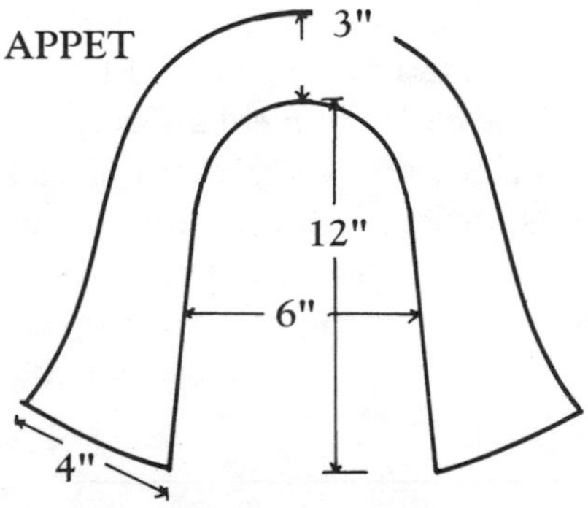

LADY IN A WIMPLE
(SEE TEXT)

CONE HAT
WITH APPET

12"

6"

4"

outer edge of the hood, known as the mantle, to fall properly over the shoulders, insert a quarter-circle-shaped wedge of cloth into the mantle at the gore point indicated in the diagram. The mantle can be made as long or as short as desired. It can hang from just below the edge of the shoulder to just above the elbow. The bottom edge of the mantle can be ornamented with shaped dags, shown in the dag illustration later in this chapter.

The entire hood, with the exception of the liripipe, should be lined with a matching, coordinating, or contrasting color. Those at the upper end of the market would have been likely to have the lining in a contrasting color.

The liripipe is made from a separate piece of cloth sewn into the hood at the back of the head. The liripipe should be made from a single piece of cloth seven inches wide and as long as you want it to be. After it has been attached to the hood, lightly stuff the liripipe with cotton batting or small scraps of soft fabric, to help it retain its round shape. Do not overstuff the liripipe, or it will not drape properly.

Women's hoods should not have a liripipe and were often worn open and turned back as shown in the illustration.

Monk's Cowl. Monks' hoods, properly known as cowls, were fuller than the hoods worn in secular society. Like the hood, the cowl can be made from a single piece of cloth folded along the top seam or from two separate pieces sewn together. Cut the cowl into a forty-inch-radius semicircle or two quarter circles. Mark and cut out the shaded, wedge-shaped area. Sew around the edges of the wedge-shaped cut. Next, sew together the lower twenty-two inches of the front of the cowl, leaving an eighteen-inch opening for the face. The bottom edge of the cowl may be seamed or left ragged, but it should not be cut in decorative dags. The cowl may be lined, but if the cloth is sufficiently heavy, it is not necessary.

Robin Hood Cap. There are several versions of this wonderfully pointy men's hat, which we are calling the Robin Hood cap, but this is the simplest to make. To provide sufficient body for the snout of the cap to stand out in front of the face without sagging, consider making the cap from medium-weight leather. The cap can be made from two pieces of material sewn together along the two top seams or from a single piece folded along one of the seams and sewn along the other. When you are sewing the rear seam, bear in mind that

the long portion of the seam should be sewn on the inside of the hat, and the short, two-and-a-half-inch vertical seam should be sewn so it is exposed on the outside of the hat. This will allow you to turn up the brim of the hat without having any visible seams.

The entire hat should be lined in a coordinating or contrasting color of fabric. When the hat is finished, turn up the brim along the dotted lines shown in the diagram. You may want to tack the edge of the brim to the hat with a few stitches to hold it in place.

Women's Cone Hat with Appet. Make the body of the hat from heavy construction paper or light-weight tag board. Shape a cylinder with an opening circumference of about twenty-three inches. This cylinder should sit on the head so it comes to the hairline in the front and falls to the base of the skull in the rear. The top of the cylinder, the end at the rear of the head, should have a circumference of approximately eighteen inches.

When the cylinder fits the head comfortably, glue, tape, or staple it together. Trim the front edge of the cylinder so it fits comfortably around the ears. Next, cut a circle of the same material that will fit onto the top opening—the small end—of the cylinder. Tape it securely in place. Cover the entire cylinder with inexpensive velvet or felt, wrapping the material around the front edge of the hat so the edge of the construction paper does not show. You may want to sew a few tiny loops of string or cloth ribbon inside the hat so it can be attached to the hair with hairpins.

Next, cut the appet, the horseshoe-shaped piece shown in the diagram, from the same material you used for the body of the hat. Trim the inner edge of the appet so it lays flat along the front edge of the hat. Cover the appet with a contrasting color material, either linen or satin. Now sew the inner edge of the appet to the front edge of the hat from a position just above one ear, around the forehead, and down to just above the opposite ear. Gently shape the bottom ends of the appet so they flare out slightly to lie on a plane with the front of the face.

Wimple and Veil. The wimple is so simple to construct that there is no need to provide pattern diagrams. Simply cut two squares of lightweight fabric thirty inches square. The first piece, the wimple, is fitted under the chin and tied, or pinned, at the top of the head. The second piece, the veil, is positioned on top of the head so one edge falls about three-fourths inch above the eyebrows. Smooth the edge of the veil

Cloak
(Women and Men)

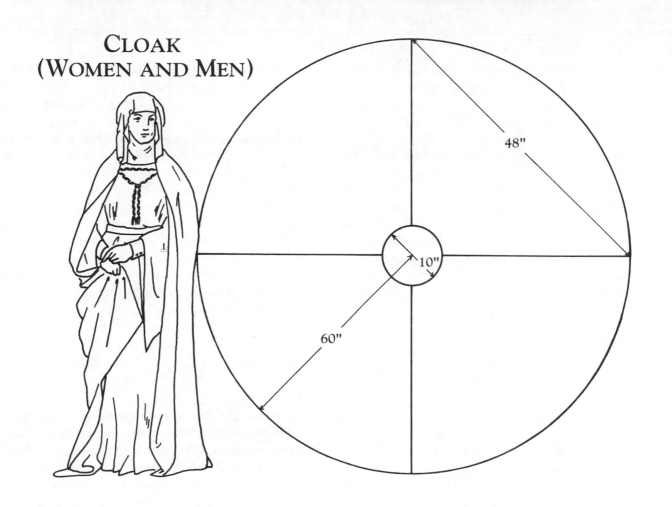

Dag Designs

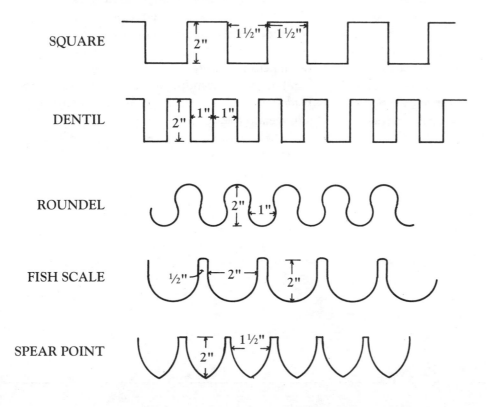

SQUARE

DENTIL

ROUNDEL

FISH SCALE

SPEAR POINT

against the forehead, tucking or pinning the natural pleats that form at the temples behind the edges of the wimple.

CLOAK

The cloak was the only outer coat of the Middle Ages. Cloak material could range from lightweight for spring, summer, and early fall to very heavy wool for winter use. Many women had a hood sewn onto the cloak, and men usually depended on a hood or hat for head protection. Whether the cloak was lined and the expense of the material used in its construction were determined by the social status and wealth of the owner. Most reenactment cloaks are cut from heavy wool blankets, such as old army blankets. They are as warm as you are likely to need, and the weave is coarse enough to pass for medieval wool. You will need to find several blankets with identical coloring to ensure that the segments of the cloak match.

Like the mantle, the full-length cloak is no more than a large circle of cloth with a hole for the head and an open seam so it can be thrown over the shoulders. Because of the amount of material required to make a full-circle cloak, it is necessary to cut four sections and sew them together. The cloak in the illustration is five feet in length. This should work for a wearer between the heights of five foot, seven and five foot, ten. For wearers who fall outside this range, the length of the cloak will have to be adjusted accordingly. If you prefer a knee-length cloak, it can probably be made from two army blankets, rather than four, each blanket forming a half circle.

When the cloak sections are cut, sew them together, leaving one seam open so the cloak can be thrown around the shoulders. Hem the edges, and line the cloak if you choose. You may want to consider attaching a hood. The cloak may be held together at the neck with string ties sewn to the cloak or with a large, decorative pin.

BELTS

Both men and women wore belts during the fourteenth century. Most full-length cotehardies were belted at the waist for both men and women. If a man was wearing a fitted, crotch-length cotehardie, he would more than likely wear his belt around his hips—probably to show that he was still slim enough to do so. The only time a woman would wear her belt at the hips would be if she was wearing a surcoat with huge arm openings on top of the cotehardie or a very form-fitting kirtle. Again, this is a style mostly reserved for those who are comfortable showing off as much of their figure as possible. Belts in the fourteenth century were about two inches in width and frequently covered with metal plates that nearly obscured the belt itself.

JEWELRY

Women might wear a cross or jewel on a delicate neck chain, and men of noble rank might wear a collar of maintenance, a large, heavily ornamented chain worn like a necklace, shown on the figure of the man in a full-length cotehardie. Rings, inset with family crests and precious and semiprecious stones, were always popular. Otherwise, jewelry was kept at a minimum.

KNIVES AND SWORDS

Military men routinely carried broadswords on their left side at all times. All men above the rank of peasant carried a dagger on their right side. When attending a great feast, an eating knife would be worn by all persons, regardless of social rank or sex. Thus, a military man attending a feast would wear three blades: a sword and eating knife on the left side and a dagger on the right.

CHAPTER 16

CHECKLIST

THREE MONTHS (OR MORE) AHEAD OF TIME

These should be done pretty much in the order listed below.

1. When. Select the time of year you want to hold your medieval feast. This will allow you to determine whether any of it can take place outdoors, what sort of games to plan for, and the kinds of food that will be most appropriate. If you are planning to have your feast during the holiday season, it is often wise to hold it over Twelfth Night (January 5) rather than just prior to Christmas, when many people have family and work commitments. If you are planning to hold a summer feast, June or September would be best; a lot of people go on vacation during July and August, and these months are often too hot to be dressed in medieval clothes.

2. How Many. Decide on the number of people you want at your medieval feast. If you are planning the feast for a church or civic organization or as a wedding, you may be looking at a sizable number of guests. Once you have determined the approximate number of people, you can start looking for an appropriate space in which to hold your feast and figuring out rough estimates on the amount of food you will need to buy.

3. Who Else. Before you go too far with the planning, be sure you can get all the help you need to put on your feast. Once you have determined the approximate number of guests you will be having and whether it is to be held indoors or out, or both, you can begin to figure out how many people it will take to help run the feast, the kitchen, and any games you have planned.

You will probably need help making the decorations and building any special equipment necessary for outdoor games. Although you won't need kitchen help until the week before the feast, you should start lining up competent people to help with the kitchen work now. Always get more help than you need; some will fade away just when you need them most, and the amount of work is always greater than you think.

4. Where. Locate a space in which to hold your feast. If it is to be in your home, determine whether it is going to be in the dining room, basement, garage, or whatever. If the feast is to be held in a church, club, or community center hall, the size of this space will probably help determine how many people you can have at the event. If you must hire a hall for the occasion, keep in mind what it is you are trying to recreate when you look at halls. An old barn can be made to look more appropriately medieval than a starkly modern banquet center with a nine-foot-high ceiling. Assembly halls in Victorian Gothic churches are about the best type of space you could ever hope to find; most cities of any size probably have at least one or two such churches that would be glad to rent out their hall.

You will also need accommodations for ancillary activities. If you are going to have outdoor activities, is there space attached to the hall, or at least in very close proximity, that you can use? Is there a place where people can change into their medieval clothes? Some people will insist on changing at the party, and if there are outdoor games, some will want to change clothes or clean up afterward. And above all, be sure there is a kitchen adequate to your needs.

5. Extras. If you are planning to hire any ancillary help—musicians, caterers, or whatever—now is the time to do so. If you are having the food catered, look for caterers who are willing to make medieval food from the recipes that you provide. Some caterers only serve from their own list of foods; others will insist they can do a medieval feast and you will discover too late that they are including potatoes and chocolate cake on the menu.

Finding good medieval entertainers, such as musicians, singers, jugglers, and fire eaters, can be difficult in some areas, but it is not impossible. A good place to start is local colleges and universities. Most of them have student medieval groups, some of whom can be hired for a nominal fee to help in the kitchen, and who will be glad to give advice, and many more have choral societies that perform medieval music; most of them also have a medieval dance group who can be hired to coach your guests. If there are superior church choirs in your area, they may be able to put together a small group of singers to perform medieval choral music. Through your search for singers and other forms of help, you are likely to run across musicians who can play medieval instruments, jugglers, and other entertainers.

Once you have settled on a space and determined how many people you can accommodate, arrange to rent any necessary tables, tablecloths, and seats. You may want to make special arrangements for platters and drinking vessels. Nothing looks less medieval than a table full of lovely white china and pressed-glass wine goblets.

6. Who. If your feast is going to be a public affair, such as a fund-raiser held by a church or community group, you should get publicity out as soon as you have located the room in which the feast will be held. The more lead time you give people, the better your response will be. Put on as aggressive a promotional campaign as possible, with posters, radio interviews, flyers, and good old word of mouth. If it will be a private party, see number 9, below.

TWO MONTHS (OR MORE) AHEAD OF TIME

7. Food Choices. When the approximate number of guests has been determined, you need to prepare the final menu and begin making your shopping list and a list of any large pots, pans, and roasting dishes you may need. Also locate trencher boards, serving platters, and drinking vessels that will look appropriately medieval. It may seem early, but a month or six weeks from now, you will be very glad you have this nasty little job out of the way. If you are working with a caterer, you need

to give as much advance notice as possible so they can make any special arrangements necessary to accommodate your medieval menu.

8. Looking Pretty. Depending on the size of the hall you are using for your feast, you will need at least two months to prepare all the decorations and carry out any special construction necessary for the hall or games. If you are dealing with a space that is not your own, you probably will not be able to begin hanging banners and arranging furniture until a few days before the event, but you want everything ready to put in place when the time comes. This is the time to begin calling in all those people who said they would be happy to help you.

9. Please Come. If this is a private party, send out the invitations at least two months in advance. Prepare informational packets containing material on costumes, the menu, the day's activities (particularly if there are games), table manners, and anything else that seems important. These information packets will help people get into the spirit of the event. Send these out as soon as you begin getting confirmations on attendance. If people haven't answered by one month prior to the event, call them; you need to know if they are coming, and they need to know what to expect.

Especially if this is to be a wedding, Christmas, or Twelfth Night affair, two months' advance notice is not out of line. Not only do you need to be relatively sure that people have not made other plans before they heard about your feast, but they will need time to pull together a costume and get excited about the feast. You may want to include a schedule of the day's activities, particularly if this is more than a dinner party. You, your assistants, and your guests should all know exactly what to expect and when.

10. Getting Dressed. Prepare your own costumes now. The larger the number of people for whom you are responsible, the bigger this job is, so get this done in advance. If you are not experienced with a needle and thread or have more than two or three costumes to prepare, you may want to delegate this. If you can't find anyone who can make or help you make the costumes, you can always hire someone. Don't wait till the last minute to do that, either. If you expect a significant number of people at your feast, the really good medieval costumes will go fast.

TWO WEEKS AHEAD

11. Checking the List. Take a day or two to confirm every item on your checklist. Be certain there is no problem with the hall, rental tables, seating, musicians, and performers. Make sure your kitchen staff is lined up and you know who is going to pick up all the groceries, and confirm the use or rental of any large pots and pans. Check that your decorating committee and the people who are in charge of the games all know what they are doing and when.

THE WEEK BEFORE

12. Pulling It Together. As soon as you can get into the space where you are holding the feast, begin decorating and arranging the furniture. You should allow at least an entire day for this, even if it is just in your own dining room. The reshuffling, moving, and hanging will take more time and energy than you imagine. When the hall is decorated, have all the games and entertainments in one place, and ensure that the games' master or mistress knows where they are and the order in which they are to take place.

13. Copying It Out. A trip to the local copy shop four of five days before the feast is a good idea. Copy song sheets, dance sheets, and game rules for each guest, or at the very minimum, make one copy for every two guests.

14. Shopping and Cooking Ahead. Reconfirm your kitchen help. Three or four days before your feast, you should do all the shopping, and some help there would be a great thing. As soon as possible after every-thing has been bought and moved to the kitchen, you need people to start cooking ahead anything that will keep for a few days.

15. Last-Minute Details. Three days before the feast, check over your entire list to be sure you haven't forgotten anything. With three days still ahead of you, you should have plenty of time to take care of any last-minute problems without going into a tailspin. Be sure all your assistants know what time they are expected on the site, know how to get there, and are ready for the big day. Don't let anyone get overexcited; be very calm and reassuring, and convince them that everything is going like clockwork and that you really appreciate their help. That's what you have to tell them, even if you are ready to pull your hair out. Whatever you do, don't let panic set in—it really will come together on the big day.

THE BIG DAY

16. Last Time Around. Early in the day, check to see that everything is in place in the hall and that the kitchen is up and running on time. Everything and everyone should be in place at least two hours before your guests begin to arrive. If everything happens on schedule, it will be a near miracle, but what really matters is that your guests and help all have the best time of their lives, and even you have managed to find time to enjoy yourself.

SOURCES

UNITED STATES
Design Toscano
1645 Green Leaf Ave.
Elk Grove Village, IL 60007
Telephone: 847-952-0100
e-mail: www.designtoscano.com
Design Toscano manufactures and markets high-quality statuary, sculpture, and tapestries. Catalog available on-line or in print.

Gabriel Guild
c/o Karen Gorst
6 North Pearle St. (404E)
Port Chester, NY 10573
Telephone: 914-935-9362
Gabriel Guild produces some of the finest available custom calligraphy and illumination and occasionally deals in original manuscript pages.

Illusion Armory
21618 N. 9th Ave.
Suite H
Phoenix, AZ 85027
Telephone: 602-582-1355

Simplicity Patterns Company, Inc.
901 Wayne Street
Niles, MI 49121-0002
Telephone: 888-588-2700
e-mail: info@simplicity.com
website: www.simplicitypatt.com
Historical costume catalogues can be ordered directly from the website.

UNITED KINGDOM

Petty Chapman
26 Halifax Old Road
Birkby, Huddersfield
West Yorkshire HD1 6EE
Telephone: 01484-512-968
Can supply both patterns for most medieval periods and a wide variety of historically correct fabric.

Kay's Medieval Clothing Patterns
4 Sandringham Drive
Welling, Kent DA16 3QU
Telephone: 0181-856-8287
Well-designed patterns from the fifteenth century supplied with easy to follow instructions.

Robin Wood
Lee Farm Cottage
Upper Booth, Edale
Derbyshire S33 72J
Telephone: 01433-670-321
e-mail: bowlturner@hotmail.com
Supplier of wooden bowls, plates, and cups. Robin is probably the best in the business.

Kit & Kaboodle
c/o Gini Newton
38 Lockwood Rd.
Wheatley, Doncaster
West Yorkshire DNI 2TT
Telephone: 01302-562-875
e-mail: gini@kitkaboodle.demon.co.uk
Carries a good line of reasonably priced table service as well as costumes.

Hightower Crafts
c/o Paul Curtis
Clwt Melyn, Pen Lon
Newborough, Anglesey
Gwynedd
Wales LL61 6RS
Carries a selection of reenforced rubber and latex weapons. If you actually want to hit each other, please use these weapons.

BIBLIOGRAPHY

Arbeau, Thoinot. *Orchésographie.* Trans. Mary Stewart Evans. Dover, 1967.

Bayard, Tania, trans. and ed. *A Medieval Home Companion.* New York: HarperCollins, 1991.

Betty Crocker's Cookbook. New York: Golden Press, 1981.

Black, Maggie. *Food and Cooking in Medieval Britain.* English Heritage, 1985.

———. *The Medieval Cookbook.* London: British Museum Press, 1966.

Braun, and Schneider. *Historic Costume in Pictures.* New York: Dover Books, 1975.

Cantor, Norman. *The Civilization of the Middle Ages.* New York: HarperCollins, 1993.

Cosman, Madeleine. *Fabulous Feasts.* New York: George Braziller, 1976.

Coulson, John, ed. *The Saints.* Bristol, England: Nicholas Adams, 1757.

Dances for Queen Elizabeth and Her Court. Dolmetsch Historical Dance Society Summer School, 1983.

Davis, Wm. Stearns. *Life on a Medieval Barony.* New York: Harper and Brothers, 1923.

Day, Brian. *A Chronicle of Folk Customs.* London: Hamlyn Books, 1998.

Diehl, Daniel. *Constructing Medieval Furniture.* Mechanicsburg, PA: Stackpole Books, 1997.

Diehl, Daniel, and Mark Donnelly. *Living Behind Walls.* 1995.

———. *Medieval Furniture: Plans and Instructions for Historical Reproductions.* Mechanicsburg, PA: Stackpole Books, 1999.

Dixon, Peggy. *Dances from the Courts of Europe.* Vol. 3. Nunsuch Early Dance, 1986.

Duby, Georges, ed. *A History of Private Life.* Cambridge, MA: Belknap/Harvard University, 1988.

Dyer, Christopher. *Standards of Living in the Later Middle Ages.* New York: Cambridge University Press, 1994.

Egan, Geoff, et. al. *Dress Accessories.* London: HMSO, 1992.

Erler, Mary, and Maryanne Kowaleski, eds. *Women and Power in the Middle Ages.* Athens: University of Georgia. 1988.

Gies, Frances, and Joseph Gies. *Life in a Medieval Village.* New York: Harper Perennial, 1990.

———. *Women in the Middle Ages.* New York: Harper Perennial, 1980.

Gies, Joseph, and Frances Gies. *Life in a Medieval City.* New York: Harper Perennial, 1981.

Hassall, W. O. *How They Lived 55 B.C.–1486.* Oxford: Blackwell, 1962.

Hieatt, Constance, Brenda Hosington, and Sharon Butler. *Pleyn Delit: Medieval Cookery for Modern Cooks.* Toronto: University of Toronto, 1979.

Holt, Richard, and Gervasa Rosser, eds. *The Medieval Town, 1200–1540.* Longman, 1990.

Houston, Mary. *Medieval costume in England and France: The 13th, 14th, and 15th Centuries.* New York: Dover Books, 1996.

Laver, James. *Costume and Fashion: A Concise History.* London: Thames and Hudson, 1992.

Lewis, K., Noel Menuge, and K. Phillips, eds. *Young Medieval Women.* Sutton, Gloucester, England: St. Martin's Press, 1999.

McLean, Teresa. *The English at Play in the Middle Ages.* Windsor Forest, Berkshire, England: Kensal Press, 1994.

Piponnier, Francois, and Perrine Mane. *Dress in the Middle Ages.* New Haven, CT: Yale University Press, 1997.

Reeves, Compton. *Pleasures and Pastimes in Medieval England*. Gloucestershire, England: Allan Sutton Publishers, 1995.

Renfrow, Cindy. *A Sip Through Time: A Collection of Old Brewing Recipes*. Self-published, 1995.

———. *Take a Thousand Eggs or More*. Vols. 1 and 2. Self-published, 1993.

Sass, Lorna. *To the King's Taste*. New York: Metropolitan Museum of Art, 1975.

Scully, Terence. *The Art of Cookery in the Middle Ages*. Woodbridge, Suffolk, England: Boydell Press, 1995.

Singman, Jeffrey, and Will McLean. *Daily Life in Chaucer's England*. Westport, CT: Greenwood Press, 1995.

Tarrant, Naomi. *The Development of Costume*. Rutledge, 1994.

Thomas, Bernard, and Jane Gingell. *The Renaissance Dance Book*. London: Pro Musica, 1988.

Virgoe, Roger, ed. *Illustrated Letters of the Paston Family*. London: Guild Publishing, 1989.

Warwickshire Country Recipes. Ravette Books, 1988.

Woolgar, C. M. *The Great Household in Late Medieval England*. New Haven, CT: Yale University Press, 1997.

Yarwood, Doreen. *Outline of English Costume*. London: Batsford, 1972

FILMOGRAPHY

The following list of films should help give you a feeling for the era as a whole: how people looked, dressed, and decorated their homes. Not all the films included on this list are from the mid-1300s, the period of our recreated feast, but even those films that take place in other time periods are informative, if only by comparison, and all of them are a lot of fun. The period of each film is indicated in the brief synopsis that follows the title.

There are certainly a lot more films about the Middle Ages than those listed below, but these are the best. We have omitted some films because they are in black and white, which gives you no sense of the colors used; others have been left out because they are simply so inaccurate, or so bad, that they will not provide useful reference or, in many cases, do not even bear watching.

Listings are by the date of the film and do not indicate any particular ranking in historical accuracy. An asterisk (*) indicates the inclusion of a wedding scene, but none of them are carried out according to medieval tradition.

Alexander Nevsky (Mosfilm, 1938) In Russian with subtitles. Set 150 years before our feast. Although it is in black and white, it is still a startlingly realistic and spectacularly executed medieval epic.

*The War Lord** (Universal, 1965) Starring Charleton Heston. Although it is set 250 years before our feast, there is a well-done medieval wedding scene here. It is also a very exciting movie and well worth watching.

The Lion in Winter (Arco/Embassy, 1968) Starring Katherine Hepburn and Peter O'Toole. Set 150 years before our feast, this is probably the most realistic-looking medieval film ever produced. It takes place at Christmastime, helpful for those planning a Christmas celebration. Hepburn and O'Toole are at their best.

Robin and Marian (Columbia, 1976) Starring Sean Connery and Audrey Hepburn. One of the best and most realistic costume set pieces. The time period is the early 1300s, the early end of our time period. Good costumes, great fun.

Ladyhawke (Warner, 1985) Starring Rutger Hauer, Michelle Pfeiffer, and Matthew Broderick. Set two hundred years earlier than our feast and pure fantasy, but great fun.

The Name of the Rose (TCF, 1986) Starring Sean Connery and Christian Slater. Set during the early years of our time period, this is one of the great medieval movies. Unfortunately, virtually everyone is a cleric, so they are all wearing monastic habits, but for those coming to the feast as priests or monks, it is great reference.

The Navigator: A Medieval Odyssey (Recorded Releases/Arena, 1988) No big-name stars. Although this is a fantasy, it is set in the time period of our feast; unfortunately, everyone in the film is a dirt-poor peasant and everything looks pretty grim. But it's an interesting film.

*Henry V** (Curzon, 1989) Starring Kenneth Branagh and Brian Blessed. Set at the end of our time period, this absolutely spectacular film provides some of the best visual reference for your party. It also contains some of the finest recreated medieval interiors ever on screen. Notice how simple and spare the sets are, but how realistic they look and feel.

Robin Hood (TCI/Working Title, 1991) Starring Patrick Bergin. By far the best of the three early 1990s Robin Hood movies. The sets and costumes are very well done and authentic to period, and since this is the same period as our recreated feast, it offers the best visual reference. The story is also quite true to many of the Robin Hood legends. This should have done far better at the box office than it did; it simply didn't have Kevin Costner's name attached to it.

*Robin Hood: Prince of Thieves** (Warner, 1991) Starring Kevin Costner. Set at the right period for our recreated feast, the costumes are good and the interior sets are fine. The problem is the story itself. You've probably seen it and heard all the jokes, but this film presents good visual reference for your feast. Just watch it with the sound turned off and you'll be fine.

*Robin Hood: Men in Tights** (TCI/Brooksfilm, 1993) Starring Cary Elwes. Again, the Robin Hood story is the right time period, and even though this is a bit of Mel Brooks fluff, it is probably better costumed than the Kevin Costner version. The wedding at the end is also fairly accurate and provides good visual reference.

Anchoress (BFI/Corsan, 1993) No big-name stars. Set in the right time period for our feast, this rather grim account of medieval life is well set and costumed and provides good visual reference.

*Braveheart** (TCF, 1995) Starring Mel Gibson. Set fifty years before our feast. Although the Scots' costumes are inaccurate (they would have been wearing kilts that came almost to their ankles), the English costumes are quite good, particularly the court clothes. There are also two versions of medieval weddings—one between William Wallace and his Scottish girlfriend, and another between the crown prince of England and a French princess—that are very good wedding reference and an accurate portrayal of how wedding ceremonies differed at various levels of society.

*Snow White: A Tale of Terror** (Polygram, 1996) Starring Sam Neal and Sigourney Weaver. Although it is set 100 to 125 years later than our feast, this unsettling version of the familiar fairy tale is spectacularly costumed and set. The characters are all fairly convincing, and despite its failure at the box office, this is an excellent medieval fantasy.

METRIC CONVERSIONS

INCHES TO MILLIMETERS

in.	mm	in.	mm
1	25.4	51	1295.4
2	50.8	52	1320.8
3	76.2	53	1346.2
4	101.6	54	1371.6
5	127.0	55	1397.0
6	152.4	56	1422.4
7	177.8	57	1447.8
8	203.2	58	1473.2
9	228.6	59	1498.6
10	254.0	60	1524.0
11	279.4	61	1549.4
12	304.8	62	1574.8
13	330.2	63	1600.2
14	355.6	64	1625.6
15	381.0	65	1651.0
16	406.4	66	1676.4
17	431.8	67	1701.8
18	457.2	68	1727.2
19	482.6	69	1752.6
20	508.0	70	1778.0
21	533.4	71	1803.4
22	558.8	72	1828.8
23	584.2	73	1854.2
24	609.6	74	1879.6
25	635.0	75	1905.0
26	660.4	76	1930.4
27	685.8	77	1955.8
28	711.2	78	1981.2
29	736.6	79	2006.6
30	762.0	80	2032.0
31	787.4	81	2057.4
32	812.8	82	2082.8
33	838.2	83	2108.2
34	863.6	84	2133.6
35	889.0	85	2159.0
36	914.4	86	2184.4
37	939.8	87	2209.8
38	965.2	88	2235.2
39	990.6	89	2260.6
40	1016.0	90	2286.0
41	1041.4	91	2311.4
42	1066.8	92	2336.8
43	1092.2	93	2362.2
44	1117.6	94	2387.6
45	1143.0	95	2413.0
46	1168.4	96	2438.4
47	1193.8	97	2463.8
48	1219.2	98	2489.2
49	1244.6	99	2514.6
50	1270.0	100	2540.0

The above table is exact on the basis: 1 in. = 25.4 mm

U.S. TO METRIC

1 inch = 2.540 centimeters
1 foot = .305 meter
1 yard = .914 meter
1 mile = 1.609 kilometers

METRIC TO U.S.

1 millimeter = .039 inch
1 centimeter = .394 inch
1 meter = 3.281 feet or 1.094 yards
1 kilometer = .621 mile

INCH-METRIC EQUIVALENTS

Fraction	Decimal Equivalent Customary (in.)	Metric (mm)	Fraction	Decimal Equivalent Customary (in.)	Metric (mm)
$1/64$	.015	0.3969	$33/64$	.515	13.0969
$1/32$	.031	0.7938	$17/32$	.531	13.4938
$3/64$	.046	1.1906	$35/64$	.546	13.8906
$1/16$	.062	1.5875	$9/16$	.562	14.2875
$5/64$	.078	1.9844	$37/64$	.578	14.6844
$3/32$	.093	2.3813	$19/32$	.593	15.0813
$7/64$	.109	2.7781	$39/64$	.609	15.4781
$1/8$	.125	3.1750	$5/8$	.625	15.8750
$9/64$	.140	3.5719	$41/64$	.640	16.2719
$5/32$	.156	3.9688	$21/32$	.656	16.6688
$11/64$	.171	4.3656	$43/64$	.671	17.0656
$3/16$	.187	4.7625	$11/16$	.687	17.4625
$13/64$	.203	5.1594	$45/64$	.703	17.8594
$7/32$	.218	5.5563	$23/32$	.718	18.2563
$15/64$	.234	5.9531	$47/64$	.734	18.6531
$1/4$	.250	6.3500	$3/4$	.750	19.0500
$17/64$	.265	6.7469	$49/64$	.765	19.4469
$9/32$	.281	7.1438	$25/32$	.781	19.8438
$19/64$	.296	7.5406	$51/64$	.796	20.2406
$5/16$	.312	7.9375	$13/16$	.812	20.6375
$21/64$	.328	8.3384	$53/64$	.828	21.0344
$11/32$	.343	8.7313	$27/32$	.843	21.4313
$23/64$	.359	9.1281	$55/64$	.859	21.8281
$3/8$	.375	9.5250	$7/8$	.875	22.2250
$25/64$	.390	9.9219	$57/64$	.890	22.6219
$13/32$	.406	10.3188	$29/32$	.906	23.0188
$27/64$	.421	10.7156	$59/64$	.921	23.4156
$7/16$	.437	11.1125	$15/16$	.937	23.8125
$29/64$	.453	11.5094	$61/64$	.953	24.2094
$15/32$	.468	11.9063	$31/32$	.968	24.6063
$31/64$	.484	12.3031	$63/64$	.984	25.0031
$1/2$	.500	12.7000	1	1.000	25.4000

INDEX